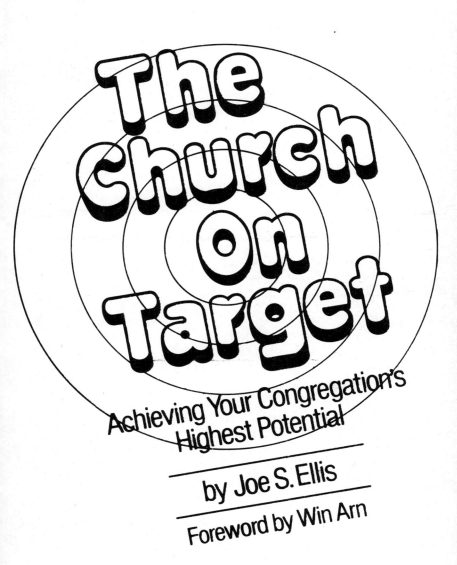

# The Church On Target

## Achieving Your Congregation's Highest Potential

by Joe S. Ellis

Foreword by Win Arn

STANDARD PUBLISHING

Cincinnati, Ohio

3019

**Library of Congress Cataloging in Publication Data**

Ellis, Joe S.
   The church on target.

   Bibliography: p.
   1. Church renewal.   I. Title.
BV600.2.E57   1986            254'.5            85-22319
ISBN 0-87403-005-6 (pbk.)

# Contents

# Foreword

It would be hard to be more excited about a book than I am about this one, from which, I believe, every Christian and every congregation can benefit.

Why is this, you ask? There are at least four reasons:

*It is a book of vision.* Page after page breathes with possibilities, with opportunities, with vision—for the work of Jesus Christ and His church. When Dr. Ellis speaks of a new era emerging within the church and the world, he is, I believe, 100% accurate. The church can no longer be doing "business as usual;" it must refocus its vision. Failure to do this will, in the years ahead, result only in decline, decay, death. This is the day for a new vision, and Dr. Ellis helps point the way.

*It is a book based on Biblical foundations.* Many books on church growth today lack such Biblical foundations, but without them, church growth does not happen. Not so of this book, which finds its springs of life in Scripture. Focusing particularly on the parable of the talents, the author brings new depth from the inspired text. This exegesis is not in isolation, but it is interpreted and applied to our world, our community, our church, our lives. The reader completes each chapter not only more knowledgable, but spiritually refreshed and invigorated.

*It is a book of strategy.* This is not a book for ivory-towered theoreticians. It is a book for individual Christians, church leaders, entire congregations who are serious about making disciples and being faithful and who realize their opportunities and potential. Yes, I agree with Dr. Ellis when he tells us that we must be goal oriented, we must plan an effective strategy, and that excuses are unacceptable, lack of productivity inexcusable.

Again, we are not just talking theory—step by step, we are led through the darkness into the light. Would that every official church board use a portion of each meeting to study a chapter of this book and apply it to their situation!

*It is a practical book.* Christians and congregations will find numerous applications for their lives and for their churches. A thoughtful reading and discussion of these chapters will have groups saying, "Yes, we can do this," or "Here is an opportunity we should take advantage of." Individuals will begin to differentiate between "busy work" and Kingdom work, between church work and disciple-making. Those who apply what they have read will look back on the purchase of this volume as one of their greatest investments. In Dr. Ellis's references to *The Master's Plan for Making Disciples* and other resources, there are "gold mines" for hands-on material for churches to get started in growth.

This book is really a mandate for action. It rings true. Its message should be widely read, discussed, understood, and applied until it permeates and penetrates every Christian . . . every group . . . the total congregation. This mandate is for each of us to see the mission and ministry of the church—a mandate that demands action!

*Dr. Win Arn, President*
*Institute for American Church Growth*

# Introduction

A shift of viewpoint, even a small one, can be critical for Christians and churches today. Let me illustrate.

On the campus of Cincinnati Christian Seminary, we have recently constructed a new multi-purpose building. We are located on a hill overlooking downtown Cincinnati; city officials are cautious about new construction on the hills because of some landslides in the past. Building codes are strict, requiring us to sink a row of pilings deep into the ground across the crest of the hill to buttress the new building's foundation. Great holes were drilled down to bedrock and filled with steel-reinforced concrete.

After the first pouring, the inspector refused to approve it. The pilings were not in the right place! The surveyor, in "shooting" his line, was a fraction off target. The first piling was all right, but 300 feet down the line, the last piling was many feet off course. The sighting had to be redone and new pilings placed. We now have a double row of reinforcements. If that building ever moves, the whole city had better look out!

I am trying to help Christians and churches change their direction. Using Jesus' Parable of the Talents, I hope we can make some slight but significant shifting of viewpoint in the direction of Biblical intentions—knowing that not too far down the way a small change can make some tremendous differences.

I address preachers, elders, deacons, Sunday-school teachers, youth workers, musicians, and church members in general, as well as Bible college and seminary students and faculty members. I urge that you prayerfully think through these matters and discuss them with others. Classes and study groups may find this book a resource to help them achieve a productive sharpening of focus in thought and labor to the glory of Jesus Christ.

As you read this book, keep a "bi-focal" attitude, with one eye on personal application and the other on its meaning for your congregation.


*Dr. Joe S. Ellis*
*Cincinnati, Ohio*
*January, 1985*

# The Parable
# of the Talents

CHAPTER 1

# Jesus Speaks to Us

We stand on the threshold of what may be the most important time for the church in the last twenty centuries. Just ahead awaits perhaps the greatest opportunity ever for the world-changing progress of the kingdom of God.

## Scripture Themes

During the reformation in Europe, Scriptures dealing with faith and the grace of God fueled the mighty progress of the revitalizing church. They were uniquely appropriate for that special moment and the dynamics that were operating.

When the restoration movement emerged in America, the texts that rose to the surface were those in which Jesus prayed for the unity and solidarity of His church in order that the world might believe in Him and be saved. Such texts galvanized the movement into magnificent accomplishments.

A new era is now emerging within the church and in the world around it. A movement like those turning points of the past is under way. Across America and around the world churches and individual Christians are reaching a new level of vitality, conviction, and bold faith. Some who have been in the doldrums of inertia are erupting into vigorous evangelism and growth. Christian leaders are looking at the task of the kingdom with clearer eyes and higher levels of determination. They are making bold, hard plans that stretch their faith.

God is doing truly great things through such people, readying them for a magnificent future of achievement in His enterprise. The next two decades could be the most fruitful, the most exciting, the most electrifying in the entire 2000-year history of the church.

The Scripture that could bring this coming age to reality might well be a parable of Jesus.

## The Parable of the Talents

Again, it will be like a man going on a journey, who called his servants and entrusted his property to them. To one he gave five talents of money, to another two talents, and to another one talent, each according to his ability. Then he went on his journey. The man who had received the five talents went at once and put his money to work and gained five more. So also, the one with the two talents gained two more. But the man who had received the one talent went off, dug a hole in the ground and hid his master's money.

After a long time the master of those servants returned and settled accounts with them. The man who had received the five talents brought the other five. "Master," he said, "you entrusted me with five talents. See, I have gained five more."

His master replied, "Well done, good and faithful servant! You have been faithful with a few things; I will put you in charge of many things. Come and share your master's happiness!"

The man with the two talents also came. "Master," he said, "you entrusted me with two talents; see, I have gained two more."

His master replied, "Well done, good and faithful servant! You have been faithful with a few things; I will put you in charge of many things. Come and share your master's happiness!"

Then the man who had received the one talent came. "Master," he said, "I knew that you are a hard man, harvesting where you have not sown and gathering where you have not scattered seed. So I was afraid and went out and hid your talent in the ground. See, here is what belongs to you."

His master replied, "You wicked, lazy servant! So you knew that I harvest where I have not sown and gather where I have not scattered seed? Well then, you should have put my money on deposit with the bankers, so that when I returned I would have received it back with interest.

"Take the talent from him and give it to the one who has the ten talents. For everyone who has will be given more, and he will have an abundance. Whoever does not have, even what he has will be taken from him. And throw that worthless servant outside, into the darkness, where there will be weeping and gnashing of teeth."

(Matthew 25:14-30)

## A Parable for Our Time

This passage is one of a cluster of parables in Matthew 24 and 25, all of which are directed to contemporary Christians—*to us.* We are the immediate object of His exhortations.

We can be sure of this because of the common framework shared by all the parables. In each of them a master is temporarily absent and then returns. All the parables deal with how the servants are to conduct themselves while the master is away. When Jesus delivered these parables, the time was approaching for Him to leave His disciples. Shortly afterward, He returned to Heaven, where He is now and will remain until His return to earth.

In one sense, Jesus is not gone. Although physically absent, He is truly in the world today. Through the Holy Spirit He lives in His people as individuals and He inhabits their collective identity, the church. The physical body in which He lived here on earth for 30-some years is gone, temporarily, but He is not absent. We are the body through which He continues His work. Even in that physical sense He is going to return, but in the meantime He is present *in* us and *among* us.

Nevertheless, we understand what He meant in the parables by the concept of the master going "away." These parables address our situation. The Master is away; He has given us instructions; He is going to come back and call us to account.

One of the parables in the cluster emphasizes that the servants must not become careless in the way they live while the Master is away (Matthew 24:36-51).

Another parable says that the Master's servants ought to maintain a sense of expectation, ready at all times to meet Him, because He might return unannounced at any moment (Matthew 25:1-13).

A third parable says that while the Master is away, His servants must care about the problems and needs of others. When we care for others, He said, we care for Him. To neglect others is to neglect Him (Matthew 25:31-46).

All these teachings strike home with serious implications for Christians and churches today. But the Parable of the Talents may be the most crucial of all. It provides a powerful way of looking at our relationship to Christ. While He is away, He says, we are to take responsibility for bringing His mission—His task, His cause—to fulfillment.

## Summary

In this timely parable, Jesus speaks to us, His servants today. He tells us the following principles of the kingdom:

- Jesus, the Master, is temporarily "away."
- We are His servants.
- He has an enterprise in the world, and it is of the highest importance.
- He has put that enterprise in our hands for us to conduct during His absence.
- He defines faithfulness as maximum productivity, and unfaithfulness as lack of productivity.

CHAPTER 2

# The Nature of the Enterprise

Exactly what is the enterprise that the Master has entrusted to our management? We dare not approach God's work with vague generalizations. The nature of our task must be clear in our minds.

Authors Arn, McGavran, and Arn point out that before one can ask, "What is the basic purpose of the church," one must address an even more basic issue:

> If we believe the church to be the Body of Christ, the Household of God, and if we see the church existing in this world to do the will and accomplish the purpose of God, we need to ask: "What is *God's* will and purpose for His people and His church?"[1]

## God's Purpose

### The World As God Intended It

God wove into the design of creation a specific set of values and principles whereby the world and human life would operate.

The natural laws, like gravitation, are easiest for us to understand because they are observable and are subject to scientific investigation. We learn to work within these laws, but we cannot change them. They are built into the very nature of creation.

The moral, psychological, social, and spiritual laws are no less a

15

part of reality than the natural laws. If we violate them, we will suffer the consequences as surely as if we violate the law of gravitation. These laws deal with the way we conduct our lives, the attitudes we hold, the values that guide us, the way we think, and the way we relate with our environment, each other, and God.

God's design included a daring proposition; He chose to make human beings creatures of free choice. He ordained that our relationship with Him be voluntary, intimate, and collaborative—the relationship of friends or partners. God would reason with us, and we would make an intelligent response of trust and obedience. In that relationship, God put the first two humans in charge of Eden.

When creation was operating according to design, God declared it "good." What marvelous cargo is carried in that one small word! The Creator meant, "It is functioning as planned. All is in harmony." Here was the ultimate of well-being. Everything that makes for life's highest good (of which we now have but tantalizing, fleeting examples) was fully and perfectly operating. In the light of this original goodness, we should be struck all the more by the tragedy of things as they have become.

## Satan's Subversion

Satan entered the scene with a counterfeit set of principles. He introduced his counter-system of thought, attitudes, and conduct—his perversions of the inner person, the social person, and the spiritual person. That counter-system can seem appealing and even logical. But counter to God's style of dealing with people, Satan's is one of subtlety, deception, and manipulation. He will, if possible, coerce and bring us into bondage.

Choosing Satan's counter-system is sin. It began when our earliest forebears made that fatal choice. Through the first sin, distortion, destruction, and deception entered the world. Human life was attacked by guilt, pain, stress, failure, competition, anxiety, sickness, and death. It was thrown out of harmony with the creation design. Even physical creation was like a train off the track.

There came a time when I, as a matter of choice, made an error similar to that of Adam. By deliberate decision I chose Satan's counter-system. At that point I was alienated from God; I became guilty and subject to condemnation. Sin gave Satan grounds to accuse me before God and bring me into bondage.

The world is now a mixture that reflects both the glory of the Creator's design and the wreckage produced by Satan's subversion. For the time being, Satan is the prince of this world. He presides over the chaos. His principles are assumed to be reality by the deceived masses whose lives are distorted by them.

We have broken ourselves against God's laws—natural, psychological, social, moral, and spiritual. All our efforts to solve our problems, to put the world in order, have been futile. From the human point of view, the situation is hopeless.

## God's Solution

Through the ages God had a plan for returning His alienated creation to himself. He would take away the wreckage and restore His original design, and He would do so without violating His own principles, without capitulating to Satan.

Jesus himself was the plan of God. In Jesus, He would begin restoring all things to the way He intended them to be.

The primary function of Jesus was that of Redeemer. He became our substitute and took upon himself our sin, our guilt, and our death, thus breaking Satan's claim upon us and renewing our relationship with God.

The Son of God became the Son of Man in order that the sons of men might become the sons of God. He rescues us from guilt and condemnation and restores us to life as God designed it to be. When we become Christians, we leave our old lives behind. As new creatures, we are reconciled to God and we are being reconciled to God's original intention.

For the present, two categories of people make up the world. Some are of the dominion of Satan, of the world as it became through sin. Others are of the dominion of light, God's kingdom restored.

The church is made up of people who are subject to Christ as Lord and are no longer in rebellion, no longer living according to their own wishes or according to Satan's system.

Jesus came as the new Adam, first of a new creation. God's design for humanity was vindicated as Jesus lived it out perfectly and became the prototype of a new race in whom God's design for life is reinstated. The church is the first installment of a new creation, God's alternative to the wreckage the earth has become. It is the new Eden—reconciled to God, set in order according to the original design, and functioning by the principles rooted in the very foundation of the world.

Its mandate is to grow. God intends that the church progressively fill the world so that re-creation moves forward. The colony of the redeemed exists to gather more and more people until, as Scripture says, "The kingdom of the world has become the kingdom of our Lord and of his Christ, and he will reign for ever and ever" (Revelation 11:15).

*This is God's enterprise in the world!* Christians sometimes pray and fret over details of the will of God. But we know what His will is in its most important aspect: the expansion of His kingdom.

## Jesus' Commission

The nature of God's enterprise becomes more sharply defined when we look at the Great Commission Jesus gave His disciples:

All authority in heaven and on earth has been given to me. Therefore go and make disciples of all nations, baptizing them in the name of the Father and of the Son and of the Holy Spirit, and teaching them to obey everything I have commanded you. And surely I will be with you always, to the very end of the age. (Matthew 28:18-20)

The Commission is an imperative statement—a command. The central imperative verb of the Commission, as most fully stated in Matthew, is *"make disciples."* Making disciples is *persuading the people of the world to become committed followers of Jesus and responsible members of His growing kingdom.*

Donald McGavran, one of this century's greatest advocates for the Commission, emphasizes the importance of the exact words used in the phrase *all nations.* In the original language the words are *panta* (all) *ta ethne* (peoples). All peoples are to be brought into discipleship to Jesus and embraced in God's new creation, the church. That includes the unreached peoples of America—minorities, ethnics, overlooked geographical pockets of people—as well as the rest of the world.

The Commission also includes other verb forms, all of which are participles that gain their strength from the imperative around

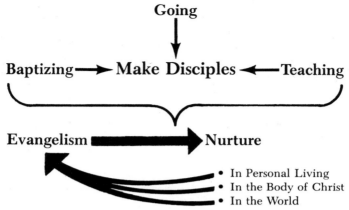

Figure 2-1. The Great Commission

which they cluster. The participles are *going, baptizing,* and *teaching.*

Together these elements form a magnificently complete statement of God's enterprise in the world. We, as individual Christians and as the church, are to make disciples of all the peoples of the world—that is, going to them and baptizing them (evangelism), and then teaching them (the nurture of Christians).

## Evangelism and Nurture

Evangelism and nurture are interdependent. They form a mutually reinforcing cycle. When winds start reinforcing one another in a common circular direction, a tornado is born, and it sweeps over the land. The church of the first century was a transforming tornado, and the whole world felt its effect. Christianity "turned the world upside down" (Acts 17:6, KJV) and changed its direction to this very day.

Nurture is an internal process to the church; evangelism is an external one. Nurture deals with the quality of the Christian's life and the quality of life among Christians; evangelism is the impact of the individuals and the corporate church on the world outside.

Evangelism deals with salvation—forgiveness of sin, reconciliation to God, transferring from Satan's kingdom to God's. Nurture deals with restoring the details of the Christian's thought and action to working order according to God's intention.

Evangelism is faulty if it does not incorporate converts into the body of Christ, where they grow and become responsible citizens of the kingdom. Nurture is misdirected if it does not break out into serious, intentional evangelism.

People ask me whether it is more important for the church to reach new people or concentrate on building up the members it already has. My standard answer is "Yes." *Both* are imperative. I give the same answer to questions about whether it is more important to plant new churches or work to build up existing churches. The answer is the same to the question about whether we should focus our attention at home or abroad.

We don't have to make choices between elements that are part of the whole Commission. We must not excuse lack of growth by claiming we are building "quality." We build counterfeit quality if it does not evangelize, if it does not anguish over the lost, if it does not urgently find ways to fulfill God's evangelistic mandate.

There is no man, woman, or child in the world that God does not want brought into discipleship to Jesus. None of our neighbors, family members, or friends are so good that they do not need to become followers of Jesus. No person in the world is so abhorrent that God does not want him won. If God had His way, the church of Christ would spread until it embraced the entirety of the globe. That requires massive evangelism.

Likewise there is no area of His people's lives that He does not want to transform and restore to His design. That requires massive and serious nurture. And nurture consists of at least three great areas of concern: living in Christ, living in the body of Christ, and living in the world.


## Elements of Nurture


### Living in Christ
Christianity is not just a matter of continuing to be the same person I have always been with church membership tacked on. It is a matter of becoming, in Christ, a new and different person. It is a matter of complete reorientation in which I rethink everything in the light of God's principles.

The church is not the world made a little better. It is a completely different order, a great alternative. We cannot count on our former experience to guide us here. We are new creatures.

When a baby is born, it has to learn from the beginning everything there is to know about life. Likewise, no one enters the kingdom of God full grown. One begins the Christian life as a babe in Christ, learning from scratch about this new life and progressing toward maturity bit by bit. We must relearn what God intends for every aspect of our temperaments, thoughts, attitudes, wills, values, words, and conduct. We submit to God's ways in order to be transformed into the likeness of Jesus, who exemplified God's design for human life.

The Bible is God's handbook for life, describing the way we are designed to function. As we appropriate its directions, life is progressively returned to working order in the way we think, the way we talk, the way we act.

### Living in the Body of Christ

A second concern of nurture is helping Christians live together in the body of Christ, the church. The church may be thought of as a colony, as this concept prevailed in the early days of the church. Philippi, for example, was a colony of Rome. The people there dressed like Romans and observed Roman time, lifestyle, and custom. They lived by Roman law and had all the privileges of Rome. It was as though a piece of Rome had been broken off and transplanted in a foreign country. That must have been the understanding of the Philippian Christians when Paul urged them to live according to the pattern he had given them and reminded them, "Our citizenship is in heaven" (Philippians 3:20).

The church is a colony of Heaven on earth. Christians must function together, not the way ordinary human beings do, but as citizens of Heaven. Relationships in the church are not just earthly relationships made a little less corrosive; they are to be of an entirely different kind. It takes deliberate effort to learn how to function this way.

Christians must also *contribute* to the life of the body of Christ. Every member of the church must function and make his contribution to its success in God's enterprise. Otherwise, he is like a cancer cell, which lives for itself at the expense of the body.

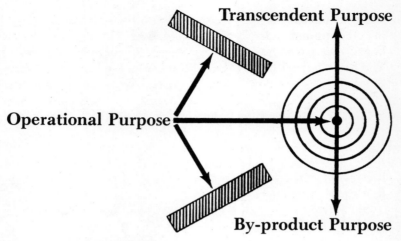

Figure 2-2. *The Law of Indirection*

### Living in the World

The Christian must also live as God's agent to the world around him. Ambassador is a Biblical word for this role. The Christian seeks ways of best representing God in his family, his job, his community, and his country. He is seeking above all to bring others into discipleship with Jesus.

When Jesus came into the world, it was God's "D-Day," on which He established His beachhead in Satan's domain. From that moment the liberation operation has gone forward. The church is here to penetrate to the uttermost parts of the earth, freeing the captives and restoring them to fellowship with God and to life.

## The Law of Indirection

Some people object to the statement that the purpose of the church is to grow in quantity and quality. The real purpose of the church, they insist, is to bring glory to God. Other people insist that the real purpose of the church is to make the world a better place by meeting human needs and attacking social inequities.

Many Christians do need to give more attention to these concerns. The question is one of priorities and strategies.

I apply to this dilemma the "law of indirection," which says that some objectives can be reached only indirectly by means of achieving other primary objectives. Happiness, for example, follows this law. Persons who set out to achieve happiness seldom attain it. The only route to happiness is by way of doing other right things.

## The Objective: to Glorify God?

Bringing glory to God is a transcendent objective best achieved by carrying out the operational purpose He has assigned us. Otherwise, bringing glory to God is an undefinable goal, and those who exalt that goal do not seem to know exactly how one goes about it. Sometimes people think they have fulfilled God's purpose when they have huddled together and whipped up spiritual (emotional?) froth. But Jesus said God is glorified as His commissioned work is carried out by His people:

> This is to my Father's glory, that you bear much fruit, showing yourselves to be my disciples (Matthew 15:8).
> I have brought you glory on earth by completing the work you gave me to do (Matthew 17:4).

God is never more greatly glorified than when people are swept into the kingdom and transformed.

## The Objective: Social Improvement?

Church growth authors argue from experience as well as logic that the objective of social improvement is best approached by the church indirectly, as a by-product of carrying out the operational purpose God has given it. That does not mean such a by-product is unimportant. It does mean that you cannot get to it without going by the specified route.

R.E.O. White illustrates the way the church indirectly achieves social reform by setting itself to accomplish its primary goal:

> Society tries to defeat evil piecemeal, sin by sin, vice by vice, restraining, controlling, ameliorating wrong without destroying its root causes, in selfishness, wickedness, pride and lust. Christian radicalism tackles the source, proclaiming liberation through a victorious Christ. Our victory lies in being led "in the train of His triumph."[2]

Society is never more affected for good than when multitudes are evangelized and transformed. Churches should seek to attack social problems directly, but the Great Commission should come first, ahead of (but not in place of) the cultural mandate.

George Hunter speaks powerfully to this point:

> Wherever, anywhere in the world over the last 19 centuries, when the Christian movement has emphasized disciple-making, two things have happened. . . . We have made some new disciples and planted some churches, and have had a social influence out of proportion to our numbers. But whenever the Christian mission has neglected disciple-making and concentrated on other facets of Christ's work, we have not made many disciples or planted many churches and have not had much social influence either! Our social causes will not triumph unless we have great numbers of committed Christians.[3]

The book of Acts chronicles a dynamic, spreading Christianity that profoundly affected the whole character of the world. It did this not through a social revolution but as a result of a spiritual revolution: bringing the people of the world to God through Jesus Christ. The by-product effect on every facet of society was enormous! And God was never more profoundly glorified!

## Summary

God established His church to finish the work of Jesus Christ, restoring the world to His original intention. Jesus' Commission told us to make disciples of all peoples.

The enterprise of God is *more and better Christians in more, better, and bigger congregations, until the peoples of this world have become the kingdom of our Lord.* The church can best achieve its other worthy goals by striving to achieve this primary goal.

---

[1]Charles Arn, Donald McGavran, and Win Arn, *Growth: A New Vision for the Sunday School*. (Pasadena: Church Growth Press, 1980), p. 37.

[2]R.E.O. White, *Five Minutes With the Master* (Grand Rapids: William B. Eerdmans Publishing Company, 1965), p. 20.

[3]George Hunter, cited by McGavran in *Understanding Church Growth* (Grand Rapids: William B. Eerdmans Publishing Co., 1980), p. 26.

*". . . and entrusted his property to them."*

CHAPTER 3

# God's Enterprise
# —and Ours

## The Divine/Human Enterprise

**enterprise,** *n.* a project or undertaking that is especially difficult, complicated, or risky, and which involves activity, courage, and energy.

Our God has an important project in this world—a bold, difficult, hazardous task that requires energy and courage! In a runaway world, He is rebuilding a kingdom that conforms to His creation intention. He is restoring human lives to reality.

From the very beginning of the Bible, we see God working out this master plan. He has an objective to which He has committed himself unreservedly.

In Jesus, He brought His plan to a culmination. Jesus was always aware that He was here on compelling business. The focal point of His life was God's enterprise: saving the lost and restoring their lives to His design.

## Our Role

Although Jesus perfectly provided salvation, it still must be applied in every age, to every generation, in every place, to every person.

25

Implementation is the part of the task He has put into our hands to carry out. He produced salvation; we are His delivery system. He inaugurated the kingdom; we press its expansion to the point of ultimate victory.

Ray Anderson has well expressed the finished, yet not finished work of God in Christ:

> One can see the church as the process of formation by which God's purpose becomes actualized in and through the world. Jesus can cry out from the cross, "It is finished," and yet he continues to be at work through the presence and power of the Holy Spirit in the life and work of Christians in the world. . . .
>
> The mission of God in the world, broadly defined, is his work of redemption through Jesus Christ as a finished work, which is proclaimed as the gospel. Through Christ's gift of His spirit, this work which has become accomplished, continues to accomplish its purpose through the transformation of sinful persons into a new community of social and spiritual health, which is the church, the body of Christ (Ephesians 1:15—2:10).[1]

Anderson has titled his document *On Minding God's Business*. That is the essence of Jesus' emphasis in the Parable of the Talents.

In the parable, Jesus refers to us as His servants or slaves. But we are also His fellow laborers, His partners, His co-missioners. As God commissioned Him, He has commissioned us (John 20:21, 17:18). Our Master is physically absent. He will return, but in the meantime *we* are the body through which He fulfills His mission.

If *enterprise* is a useful word to describe what God is doing in the world, *entrepreneur* can describe the role He has given us: "One who organizes, manages, and assumes the risk of a business or enterprise." We must approach God's business with the attitude of entrepreneurs.

### God's Dependency

God is all-knowing, all-powerful, and ever present, full of majesty and authority. But God is also dependent upon His people. He relies on us to undertake His affairs in the world and bring them to success.

God's design includes a built-in respect for our integrity. He prefers not to intrude unbidden. Revelation 3:20 has often been assumed to be an evangelistic statement in which Christ offers salvation, but this statement occurs within the context of a communication to the church. "Here I am! I stand at the door and knock. If anyone heard my voice and opens the door, I will come in and eat with him, and he with me." Even in the lives of His own people, the church, Christ prefers not to intrude where He is not wanted. He may ask entrance, but it is up to us to invite Him in as friend to friend.

Is it too strong a word to think of God as helpless? His is a self-imposed helplessness, but by His plan, He must find persons who will provide the lips through which to speak, the hands through which to serve, the resources, strategies, and efforts through which to build His kingdom. He seeks entrepreneurs who will bring His affairs to success. He looks to us to be those people. Such a risk, to entrust us with that mission to which He has committed himself so fully—and for which no price has been too high to pay!

The salvation provided by Jesus in His death and resurrection remains unavailing until it is brought to people by other people. In Romans 10, the logic runs like this: people cannot be saved until they believe in Christ; they cannot believe until they hear of Him; they cannot hear unless they are told; they cannot be told unless we provide for it. God is depending on us.

This principle is without exception in the New Testament. The conversion of Cornelius is recorded in Acts 10. He was a God-fearing man but not yet a Christian. God intervened in his life with a vision—not to save him, but to instruct him to send for Christ's servant, Simon Peter, who would bring him the message of salvation. Peter came and declared the gospel to Cornelius and his family, and they became disciples of Jesus.

In Acts 9, the archenemy of the church, Saul, was divinely intercepted on his way to Damascus. The encounter did not make him a Christian. On the contrary, the Lord told him to go on to the city where he would be told what to do. There, a servant of Christ led Saul to faith and obedience to Christ.

Having put the implementation of His work into the hands of His people, God did not circumvent His plan, not even in those magnificent days of the early church. Why should we expect exceptions today? That is the way the kingdom was built yesterday, the way it is built today, and the way it will be built tomorrow.

# The Church as a Partnership

The kingdom of God is built in this world by two elements: the power of God and the effort of human beings or, more precisely, the power of God *through* the effort of human beings.

God's enterprise is a partnership in which He assigns us an essential role. Paul balances the divine and human roles in the growth of the church. First he uses the concept of a field under cultivation:

> What, after all, is Apollos? And what is Paul? Only servants, through whom you came to believe—as the Lord has assigned to each his task. I planted the seed, Apollos watered it, but God made it grow. So neither he who plants nor he who waters is anything, but only God, who makes things grow. The man who plants and the man who waters have one purpose, and each will be rewarded according to his own labor. For we are God's fellow workers; you are God's field (1 Corinthians 3:5-9).

Paul does not diminish the role of persons in the planting and watering. God does not make the field produce without these functions. But without God's involvement, these functions are futile. The collaboration of both is the secret to the success of the kingdom enterprise.

Jesus himself used this figure when He referred to the harvest:

> The harvest is plentiful but the workers are few. Ask the Lord of the harvest, therefore, to send out workers into his harvest field (Matthew 9:37, 38).

Like a harvest field that is ripe and in urgent need of reaping, the world is to be reached for the kingdom. If not gathered when ripe, the harvest is lost. Therefore, He urges prayer for more harvesters. Once again, God and His people are seen as collaborators.

Paul uses another figure of speech to illustrate the principle:

> By the grace God has given me, I laid a foundation as an expert builder, and someone else is building on it. But each one should be careful how he builds. For no one can lay any foundation other than the one already laid, which is Jesus Christ. If any man builds on this

foundation using gold, silver, costly stones, wood, hay or straw, his work will be shown for what it is, because the Day will bring it to light (1 Corinthians 3:10-13).

Not only do servants of Christ participate in the building of the kingdom, it is imperative that they give to the work the best of which they are capable. Paul characterizes his work as that of an *expert* builder. No haphazard workman, this servant of Christ! We may build with the magnificent quality of precious metal or splendid marble, or our work may take on a shoddy quality with hay or straw, but build we must. God, on the other hand, has provided the one and only foundation; Jesus Christ. Only the best workmanship is worthy of such a foundation!

In Ephesians 4, Paul uses yet another figure of speech—the growth of a body, of which Christ is the head. It cannot survive without Him even if it has all the other parts. But neither can a body function and grow if it consists only of a head.

From him the whole body, joined and held together by every supporting ligament, grows and builds itself up in love, as each part does its work (Ephesians 4:16).

## The Errors of Extremes

People err in two extremes regarding their role in building God's kingdom in the world. Some would assume total responsibility for the task; others would abdicate all responsibility. The first error I call *practical humanism;* the second, *pious irresponsibility.*

### Practical Humanism

The practical humanist acts as if God were not in the picture. If the church is to go forward, the humanists assume, it will be solely through their efforts, their ingenuity, their decisions, and good old Yankee know-how. They would soundly affirm the reality of God, but they often act as if God did not really exist, or at least as if He were not involved. They act as if He had given the rules and had truly gone away, leaving them to apply the rules in His absence.

Nineteenth-century philosopher Soren Kierkegaard opened a

Pandora's box of problems with his philosophy, but he also made some astute observations about the church of his day. The Danish church was in a quagmire of rationalism. He saw churchmen as content because they had the Bible shut up between pretty bindings. He described their passionless correctness, their dead orthodoxy, their impotent routines as "an impudent indecency."

Much church talk about God gives the impression of mere formality, the feeling that these people do not really believe there is such a Person and that the church is no more than a human institution.

Sometimes the voice of Jesus saying, "I will build my church," can hardly be heard amid the babble of human voices affirming, "We will build the church. Our plans, our organizations, our resources will accomplish it, and we will have it the way we want it." God is sometimes boxed out of His own enterprise by His self-centered or self-sufficient partners.

In the book of Revelation, the Lord addressed seven churches of the day. One was the church at Sardis (Revelation 3:1-3), a busy, active congregation. They had a magnificent reputation and the appearance of fabulous success. Behind the busy facade there was much human effort and ingenuity. But the Lord declared them a miserable failure and called them to repent.

Probably the greatest unexplored frontier is not space, nor the atom, nor genetics, but the promise of Jesus that if we have faith nothing shall be impossible (Matthew 17:20). We have yet to see what God might do through people who will give Him a one hundred percent opportunity to demonstrate what He can and will do.

When Paul wrote to the floundering, off-course church at Corinth, he asked, "Are you not acting like mere men?" (1 Corinthians 3:3) It was scandalous, shocking, to him that the people of Christ should act like ordinary human beings. Christians have to be more than that. They must go beyond the earthly and the mortal and function like true servants of the Master.

Psalm 127 reinforces this point. It says, "Unless the Lord builds the house, its builders labor in vain." A church may be built by human effort and ingenuity, but unless the Lord is building the church though that, we are wasting our time. It is simply a human enterprise.

## Pious Irresponsibility

The opposite extreme is equally wrong. In this case the servants of the Master act and think as if the success of God's enterprise were totally up to Him. After all, didn't He say, "I will build my church?" Don't many Scriptures ascribe its progress and success to Him? If that is the case, we don't have to worry about it. Our role is simply one of standing by to see what God is going to do.

Much of today's theology has underestimated man's role in God's plan and his freedom to affect the outcome. These views think of he future as already determined, already existing "out there," waiting for us to arrive. Nothing that we do, they say, can have much effect on it. No wonder Christians and congregations are so often inert!

God has given His people a critical role to play in His enterprise. I spoke on this subject in a congregation not long ago. Afterwards, one man was frank enough to tell me what he was thinking. He said, "I never thought of that before. I have never realized that we have so much effect on what happens in the kingdom. I always thought of God doing it all." This man, an officer who helped set the direction and program of the congregation, had honestly never realized that he or the board or the congregation had any real effect on God's enterprise.

People with this attitude act as if thought, planning, and effort on their part is somehow unncessary, perhaps even presumptuous or sinful.

> Once John Wesley received a note from a self-appointed evangelist saying, "The Lord has told me to tell you that He doesn't need your book learning, your Greek and Hebrew." Wesley replied, not too tactfully, "Thank you, sir. Your letter was superfluous, however, as I already knew the Lord has no need of my book learning, as you put it. However, although the Lord has not directed me to say so, on my own responsibility I would like to say to you that the Lord does not need your ignorance either."[2]

God is not praised by human presumptuousness on one hand or by human inertia on the other.

One night Jesus' disciples had been fishing, hauling up empty nets. Jesus came to them and told them to throw their nets on the other side of the boat. Their attitude was, "We tried that side and there wasn't anything there, but if You say so, we'll do it." So they cast their nets on that side and caught a shoal of fish that they couldn't even haul into the boat, and they were astonished. Jesus said, "Henceforth, you shall catch men" (Luke 5:1-11).

We can, if we choose, attempt to do all the work of the kingdom by ourselves. If so, we will wear ourselves out hauling up empty nets. But we can also sit complacently in the boat, nets neatly folded and empty, assuming it is God's job to produce results. However, when we cast the net as He directs and do our job diligently, He provides the result.

## The Effect of God's People on His Enterprise

Through the centuries, God's people have had an enormous effect on what God has accomplished in His enterprise. Sometimes they have had a positive effect and progress has gone forward in giant strides. At other times they have had a negative effect, bringing progress to a halt or moving in reverse.

### Biblical Examples

God led His people, Israel, out of captivity in Egypt and to the very border of the land He promised them. There they made camp and sent a party of twelve men to explore what lay before them. God had promised them the land, yet they were to go in and possess it—again, a matter of partnership.

The scouting party returned with a mixed report. They were in agreement that the land was everything they had been promised: it "flowed with milk and honey." But the land could never be theirs, they said. It was already occupied. The inhabitants were large and strong, and they were well-armed and lived in fortified cities. There was no way that Israel could take the land.

Two of the men disagreed with the majority and appealed for faith. This was God's doing, they said. It was not up to them alone; did they not remember all that God had been doing in their midst?

But the people's courage failed. They listened to the ten and turned back into the wilderness through which they had come.

For some forty years they wandered until all the adult generation, except the two men of faith, had died and been replaced by a new generation who would obey Jehovah's command: "Take possession of the land and settle in it, for I have given you the land to possess" (Numbers 33:53).

God's enterprise was set back four decades, through no fault of His, but because He allows people that kind of participation in His program. If His people hinder Him, He lets them—not because He is weak, but because He has ordained for His people the role of partner.

Scripture abounds in positive examples as well. Second Kings 4 contains the account of a divine miracle teamed with human pragmatics. The widow of a servant of God was destitute. She approached the prophet Elisha with her problem. Upon questioning her, Elisha found that the only item of value she possessed was a vessel of oil. The prophet told her,

> Go around and ask all your neighbors for empty jars. Don't ask for just a few. Then go inside and shut the door behind you and your sons. Pour oil into all the jars, and as each is filled, put it to one side (2 Kings 4:3, 4).

She did as instructed. Her sons brought the empty jars and removed them as they were filled—all from the original vessel. Finally, when there was not one empty jar left, the oil stopped flowing. When she told Elisha what had happened, he instructed her to sell the oil, pay her debts, and live on what was left.

Had she not carried out the prophet's instructions, she would have received no blessing. Had she borrowed half as many jars, she would have received half the blessing. *She* set the limits on the result. Her preparation to receive the blessing determined the extent of it.

## An Amazing Opportunity

More than any other factor, God's people themselves influence the success or failure of God's kingdom. God always wants and is capable of great results. Satan never wants great results and works against them constantly. The major difference is in God's people. Time and place affect the outcome, *but we affect it even more.*

How often the church is held back because God does not always have the kind of people to get the job done. Its progress leaps forward, comes to a standstill, or slips backward—not because God changes, not primarily because of circumstances, but more than anything else because of the characteristics of the people with whom He is working. He works with what he has. If we serve Him poorly, He waits for those who will do better.

I recently visited a three-year-old congregation. Everything about its location is wrong. It is miles from town on a poor road and all but impossible to find. Yet they cannot build fast enough to keep up with their growth, and they are currently erecting a 2500-seat auditorium. Other churches languish in the midst of favorable circumstances—all due primarily to the people through whom God is working.

Ashley Johnson was a man of great faith and great accomplishment who founded Johnson Bible College in the 1890's. His motto for his own life and for the school was summed up in three words: faith, prayer, and work. His formula was to pray and exercise faith as if everything depended upon God and to work as if everything depended upon him. Ashley Johnson understood and practiced the essence of divine/human collaboration.

Ours is a day that calls for that rare combination of divine power linked with human faith and pragmatics. And I believe that our generation is in the process of rising up and providing God the quality of lives and the effort He can use to do great things. It is not a generation like that which stood on the brink of the land of promise and failed. Even if there are giants in the land (and there are plenty of them!), God can accomplish much through our generation.

## Summary

God's work is accomplished by a combination of human and divine effort. We cannot do it without Him; He has ordained not to do it without us. We depend on each other.

If we pursue the work of the kingdom by our own wits and energies alone, we will not succeed and our work will wear us down, eroding our energies and resources. Likewise, if we fail to act responsibly, God's program will flounder. But if we work wisely, expertly, and diligently in the task Christ has given us, life and work will be exhilarating!

---

[1]Ray S. Anderson, *On Minding God's Business*. Published by the author at Fuller Theological Seminary, 135 N. Oakland, Pasadena, CA 91101, pp. 7, 12.

[2]Cited by Calvin Phillips in his inaugural address as President of Emmanuel School of Religion, October 25, 1984.

CHAPTER 4

# Jesus' Standard of Faithfulness

Stewardship is often equated with the Christian's use of financial resources. Actually this is only one application of the Biblical concept of stewardship. We are stewards of the gospel, of Christ's enterprise in the world (1 Corinthians 4:1). Our use of money is only one aspect of that trust.

The faithful steward of Christ is one who subjects his personal interests (resources, time, energy, commitment, and priorities) to the cause of Christ in order to produce maximum results. Congregations are faithful to the extent that they do the same.

## Faithfulness Defined

Jesus taught that we, His servants, are useful only as we function in that which we are supposed to do. He says, "You are the salt of the earth." Salt is supposed to function in certain ways. If it doesn't, it has no value. Likewise He says, "You are the light of the world." Light is supposed to dispel darkness. If prevented from doing so, it is useless (Matthew 5:13-16).

But no one states this principle more clearly than Jesus, when He compares us to branches and himself to the vine:

36

I am the true vine and my Father is the gardener. He cuts off every branch in me that bears no fruit, while every branch that does bear fruit he trims clean so that it will be even more fruitful. . . . No branch can bear fruit by itself; it must remain in the vine. Neither can you bear fruit unless you remain in me.

I am the vine; you are the branches. If a man remains in me and I in him, he will bear much fruit; apart from me you can do nothing. If anyone does not remain in me, he is like a branch that is thrown away and withers; such branches are picked up, thrown into the fire and burned (John 15:1-6).

In the Parable of the Talents the master returns, calls his servants to an accounting, and evaluates whether they have succeeded or failed. He finds that the servant who was entrusted with five talents has doubled it. The master declares him faithful. The servant who was given two talents has also doubled that. He also is declared faithful.

In simplest terms, Jesus defines faithfulness (or success) as accomplishing as much as possible with the resources one has. He is depending on us to be as shrewd and deliberate as we can be in order to bring His enterprise to the highest possible level of success.

Jesus qualifies this definition, however. He does not expect us to produce *more* than we can, just *all* that we can with His help. In the parable, one servant gained five units of money; another, only two. The amounts they produced were different, but the master's praise to both servants is identical, word for word. Both succeeded equally. Both were declared faithful.

Faithfulness is not measured against some arbitrary production goal. Success is not determined by how much we accomplish, but by how much we accomplish in comparison to our potential. The servant who made five talents had, from the beginning, an edge on the others. He had more to start with. But both he and the two-talent man succeeded equally in the master's eyes. When any servant of Christ, given his innate abilities and opportunities, does all he can—however much or little that is—he has succeeded.

The same standard applies to churches. One congregation may grow to the thousands and another may struggle to reach one hundred. But depending on the opportunity, the second church *may* have succeeded just as much as the first.

37

We must be careful not to underestimate our "talents" and excuse ourselves for not accomplishing all we can. If we have realistically assessed our opportunities and have produced to the maximum, we are declared faithful. In my observation, though, most people are in more danger of underestimating their potential and expecting too little than they are of setting their sights too high.

I believe we are living in a time of great possibilities and that Christ has the right to expect much of our generation. "From everyone who has been given much, much will be demanded; and from the one who has been entrusted with much, much more will be asked" (Luke 12:48).

## Unfaithfulness Defined

Now Jesus tells us what unfaithfulness on the part of His servants is: *failure to produce what we can.*

That third servant is intriguing. He is not a scoundrel or a thief. He didn't steal the money. He didn't misappropriate it. He didn't waste it. He didn't risk it. He didn't lose it. He preserved it intact! At first glance we might consider him a good man. He kept with scrupulous care what was entrusted to him. He buried it where it would be safe and guarded it.

"See, here is what belongs to you," he said, when he brought the money back to its owner. "I knew you are a hard man to please, so I have guarded it, protected it, preserved it intact. Not a penny is missing."

But the master calls him, in various translations, wicked, lazy, slothful, unprofitable, worthless, useless, unproductive, *unfaithful.* How shattering! Is there anything much worse to call him?

According to Jesus' standard, to fail we don't have to run amuck and do something dreadful. We don't have to deny the faith. We don't have to adopt some doctrinal heresy. We don't have to run off with somebody else's wife. We don't have to rob a bank. To fail as the Master's servants we don't have to do any of these things. To fail, all we have to do is *nothing!*

The Master's inescapable question is, "How much have you produced in My enterprise?" No other issue or excuse can substitute for our answer to this question.

The third servant was unfaithful because he was unproductive in the enterprise to which his master had commissioned him. His unfaithfulnes lay not in the fact that he failed to produce five talents more, or even two. His failure was that he didn't do what he could. If he had, he would have been equally as successful as the other two.

Apparently this reality has never dawned on many of the Lord's servants. Much of the Lord's best work has been done by one-talent people. They have taken the little opportunity they had and produced all they could. In some cases, the Lord has blessed their efforts until the results were truly astonishing. But many one-talent people belittle their abilities and do nothing, and even many multi-talented servants of Christ feel little remorse about following the erroneous logic of the third servant.

## A Fatal Error

God's people persistently try to redefine faithfulness in their own terms. Redefined, faithfulness can take many forms—unity, doctrinal purity, or political or social action. But most often people redefine it exactly as the third servant did—in terms of maintenance or protection rather than productivity, in terms of activity rather than results—to hide the fact that there are no results.

### The Nation of Israel

The Jewish nation into which Jesus was born illustrates this error. In the beginning, God chose that nation to be His partners in His enterprise in the world. They were to collaborate with Him in establishing His kingdom. Through them, God promised, all peoples on earth would be blessed (Genesis 22:18).

But that nation gradually redefined their role in God's scheme of things. They began to think that they had been chosen because they were worthy, that they had been blessed because they deserved it. They forgot that they had been chosen for the purpose of helping God achieve His aims, that they were blessed to be a blessing. To them, being God's people became its own end. It was a dead-end goal that led them to become a static and often contrary people, rather than accomplishers of God's enterprise.

The nation of Jesus' day failed because they redefined faithfulness. They defined faithfulness as orthodoxy rather than productivity. The scribes and Pharisees, for example, said that their job was to "build a fence round the law." They buried their trust in the ground and guarded it, so to speak, rather than putting it to work and accomplishing as much as possible.

Ironically, the Pharisees came on the scene of history as God's heroes in a time of spiritual decline and sacrilege. They were the brave few who stood their ground against paganism. It was they who provided a rallying point and led the nation in a comeback. But two hundred years later they had sunk into a maintenance mentality, defensive thinking that led to paralysis of God's enterprise.

## Christians Today

Some Christians, churches, and parachurch organizations make the same error today. They proudly herald themselves as "keepers of the faith." They defend the Bible and orthodoxy, as they understand it, with a vengeance. With powerful rhetoric they condemn heresy, as they define it, wherever they can ferret it out. Others doggedly declare that they "hold forth the word of life" (but with a kind of take-it-or-leave-it attitude).

How can we find fault with those who keep the faith or hold forth the word of life? We can't, unless those who espouse the slogans are static when it comes to producing results. We can be vigorously orthodox and yet unfaithful to God's mandate if the kingdom is not growing significantly through our committed efforts.

In an athletic contest, the best a team can hope for, if it has only a good defense, is a nothing-to-nothing tie. You can't win a game without a good offense, without scoring points. What may go down in history as the most boring basketball game of all time was played in the midwest a few years ago. The underdog team was thought to have no possibility whatsoever of winning the game, and they believed it. They played the entire game with one strategy: keep the ball away from the other team so they would score as few points as possible. Their objective was to lose by the smallest possible margin. How much better it would have been to lose by ten times as many points while playing their hearts out!

The church of Jesus Christ *must not* have this kind of mentality! The church is not here just to survive, to cut its losses, to hold the enemy at bay! It is here to win!

Paul often compares the Christian enterprise to athletics. Of himself, he said that he was not just going through the motions, not just doing warm-ups. He was fighting to win! (see 1 Corinthians 9:24; Philippians 3:14) And so should we!

## Summary

*Faithfulness,* as Jesus defined it in the Parable of the Talents, means achieving maximum results with what we have. Unfaithfulness is the failure to do so.

Historically, when God's people tried to redefine "faithfulness" to mean something else, God's purpose was not achieved and His enterprise languished.

*"For everyone who has will be given more.
. . . Whoever does not have, even what he
has will be taken from him."*

# CHAPTER 5

# Jesus' Promises

Jesus says one thing further. It is in the form of two promises:
one positive, the other negative.

## A Reward and a Warning

Jesus says that if we are faithful in producing as much as we
can, He will give us opportunities to produce still more. Faithfulness leads to greater faithfulness. Growth begets growth. God
entrusts yet more to those who have proved themselves trustworthy.

I know a church, for example, that is evangelizing rapidly.
They baptize many people every week. They are bounding ahead
in growth. Many observers ask that congregation where they find
all those people they reach with the gospel. Their answer is that
they don't have to worry about where to find the people. So many
people walk through their doors on Sunday—people who are not
Christians but who are seeking God's intention for them—that the
church is kept busy teaching and winning them. It is all they can
do to keep up with the task.

They are willing to do whatever it takes to serve the Lord's
enterprise. They build buildings as necessary. They expand pro-

grams, add worship services and Sunday-school classes, and find new ways to meet the needs of people in their community. They add salaried staff members to best use their opportunities and stimulate growth. And God is providing them more and more opportunities because they are doing all they can to take advantage of those He provides.

The negative promise (or warning) is that failure to use the opportunities we have to serve Christ's enterprise will lead to diminished opportunity.

Not three miles away from the flourishing congregation just described is the building of another church, doctrinally very much like the first. The congregation is withering away because they are too absorbed with their own self-interests to take advantage of opportunities to serve Christ's larger enterprise. Even the opportunities they have had are drying up. Unfaithfulness leads to its own undoing.

## A Law of the Kingdom

"Whoever can be trusted with very little can also be trusted with much, and whoever is dishonest with very little will be dishonest with much" (Luke 16:10).

We are dealing with an absolute law of the kingdom. In the parable, the master handed over to his servants a vast amount of wealth; but he gave them varying amounts depending on their abilities. One kind of servant used the opportunities he had and was given more because he had proved himself trustworthy. The other kind failed to use his opportunities and lost them. It is the principle of use it or lose it; use it and gain more.

I have seen small churches seize every opportunity to serve Christ's interests, forget self in seeking the success of His enterprise, and take bold risks in faith. I have seen such churches become great churches.

I have seen churches of much greater size become self-absorbed and unconcerned about their mission, unwilling to pay the price of growth. I have seen them losing their opportunities and withering, sometimes to the point of extinction.

## The Tenants

Jesus illustrated this law in a parable about the history of His nation, the Parable of the Tenants (Matthew 21:33-46).

A man who owned a vineyard put tenants in charge of it and went away on a journey. At harvest time he sent servants (the prophets) to receive his share of the produce. But instead of complying, the tenants abused the servants—beating one, killing another, and stoning a third. A second group of servants were treated the same.

Finally the owner sent his son. The tenants might mistreat the servants, he thought, but surely they would respect and obey the son. But the tenants said, "This is the heir. Come, let's kill him and take his inheritance." So they threw him out of the vineyard and killed him.

At this point in the parable, Jesus made His hearers pronounce judgment on the tenants.

> "He will bring those wretches to a wretched end," they replied, "and he will rent the vineyard to other tenants, who will give him his share of the crop at harvest time" (Matthew 21:41).

Those hearers were pronouncing judgment on themselves, and they realized it. Then Jesus concluded the parable:

> Therefore I tell you that the kingdom of God will be taken away from you and given to a people who will produce its fruit (Matthew 21:43).

True to the parable, the people took Jesus, God's Son, and killed Him. But it was also true that the kingdom was taken from the nation of Israel and given to others because it did not produce God's objectives.

Who are these "others"? Christians, the church—*us!* It has been given to us to produce its fruit!

This parable is strong; it's tough. It spoke not only to the unfaithful, failing nation, it speaks to us who are now the tenants of God in His vineyard. He has put us here to produce for Him.

I believe the kingdom of God can be "taken from" individuals and churches even today. I have seen once-great, vigorous congregations become hollow and wither away. They may continue as human organizations. Superficially, they may even seem to flourish, but not by God's standards. Their essential nature as the people of God has dissipated. I have seen once-effective servants become empty shells. Does God leave His enterprise in the hands of those that will not produce? Or will He take it away and give it to others who will?

## Two Individuals

The law holds true for individuals as well as for congregations. Take the case of a fine Christian woman, an excellent wife and mother, but considered mentally handicapped as the result of an illness. She could no longer handle household records, shop, make change, or drive a car. Her memory was "impaired" and she no longer trusted herself to hold serious conversations. The medical prognosis was that she would probably never improve.

Then her husband was tragically injured in an automobile accident. He lay unconscious in a hospital for many months before his final life functions ceased. She practically lived in the hospital during those months. There she had many opportunities to be God's minister to families in circumstances as tragic as her own. The word spread, and desperate people gravitated to this remarkable woman of faith. She became a chaplain to countless people— comforting them, reassuring them, strengthening them, weeping with them, rejoicing with them, and most of all introducing many of them to Jesus.

She used all the capacities that remained in her "impaired" condition. Laboriously she drew Scriptures and thoughts out of her memory. She expressed them in conversation only through great effort. Little by little, in her own way, she became a gifted— even eloquent—vessel in Christ's enterprise.

Through prayer and dogged determination, she came to drive her car again, manage her household well, raise her children as outstanding Christians, and even hold a job to support her family (where she continued to be an eloquent agent for Christ). In her congregation, she became a center of healing, reconciliation, strength, and faith.

How does one account for this? The woman took all the gifts and opportunities she had, diminished as they seemed. She used them to maximum advantage to grow as God's woman and as

God's agent, and God gave her more—much more—to invest for His glory. Today, she is one of the most competent and productive Christians I know!

> For everyone who has will be given more, and he will have an abundance (Matthew 25:29).

By contrast, one of the most gifted men of God I have known has scattered his interests, neglecting his opportunities to serve the kingdom. His moral and spiritual life deteriorated until he became an incompetent shell of the person he once had been, tragic in life and counterproductive to the kingdom.

> Take the talent from him. . . . Whoever does not have, even what he has will be taken from him (Matthew 25:28, 29).

## Summary

The conclusion of the parable is also a law of the kingdom: Whoever has will receive more; whoever does not have, even what he has will be taken away. If a person does not produce results for God's kingdom, God will take it away and give it to someone who will.

# Essentials
# for Success

# CHAPTER 6

# Goal-Orientation

Pablo Casals was one of the truly great musicians of all time. He was the undisputed master of the cello in his era. At age 95, Casals was still practicing six hours a day. A reporter interviewing him on that birthday asked, "The world knows that you are the greatest in your field. You're 95 years old. Why do you still practice so much?"

"I think I'm making progress," Casals answered.

He had set his heart on mastery of his art, and at 95 he was still working diligently at it.

Great achievers strive for great goals. They are people of purpose. Significant people know exactly what they are trying to accomplish, and everything they do is geared toward achieving it.

People become great Christians when they set their hearts upon becoming the best possible servants of Christ, when they set excellence of life and service as their goal, when they determine to be great achievers in God's enterprise. Churches become great when they think and act in such a fashion.

Ineffective people and churches have only vague and general goals. Far too many people—far too many churches—seem to have set their hearts on nothing. They wander aimlessly through life and operate by cliche; their only real goal is to go on existing. And their accomplishments are negligible.

# The Need for Goals

Human beings are made to be goal-oriented. I believe this is part of what it means to be "made in the image of God." Of all God's creation, only humans are capable of this Godlike quality. We alone can be deliberate partners with God in accomplishing His objectives.

Even non-Christian students of the human mind recognize that a person, in order to function fully as a human being, must have a sense of meaning, or purpose, or he cannot function. Abraham Maslow says we have a hierarchy of needs, and that our needs on one level must be satisfied before we can give attention to needs at a higher level. His theory says, for example, that man cannot focus on other concerns until survival needs are met. But Maslow found that there are people who are willing to forfeit even survival for the sake of finding meaning to life.

William Glasser says that we have two basic necessities, love and meaning. Victor Frankl has concluded that people have a "will to meaning." Lawrence Crabb, who writes from a Christian perspective, says that the two basic necessities are security and significance. All these observers are saying that everyone needs meaning or significance—in other words, a central target that makes sense of life.

Individual persons must have a goal big enough to command all the elements of life, bringing them together so that they are in balance and in harmony. The goal must also be authentic—that is, in keeping with God's intentions for humankind.

Goal-orientation is the characteristic that integrates life into a consistent whole and generates the driving power and compelling urgency for achievement. Churches must have that quality, and Christians must have it, if the kingdom is to meet the Master's expectations.

The alternative to goal-orientation is not very exciting. In Wonderland, Alice stood at the crossroads with the Cheshire cat looking on. "Which road shall I take?" she asked.

"Well, where are you going?" the cat inquired.

"I don't know," she replied.

"Well then," said the cat, "if you don't know where you are going, one road is as good as another."

Pogo, the erstwhile comic strip philosopher, is credited with a brilliant observation on life—"If you don't know where you're going, you just might end up someplace else."

"Be very careful what you set your heart upon, for you shall surely have it"—*even if it is nothing.* Most people really do get what they want if they want it badly enough.

## Biblical Examples

Goal-orientation is a characteristic of God. All through the Bible He is seen channeling everything to the single purpose of accomplishing His goal. He never wanders. Whatever happens, He channels it back on track and keeps moving toward His goal.

Jesus was the most goal-oriented person who ever lived. His life was totally focused on His reason for being here: to seek and save the lost and give His life as a ransom for many.

As a boy He stayed behind at the temple in Jerusalem and was surprised that His parents did not realize where He would be. He expected to be found involved in God's affairs.

As Jesus continued His work, King Herod became increasingly disturbed by it and began making threats. The Pharisees, who were constantly badgering Jesus, brought Him the news that Herod wanted to kill Him. How did Jesus handle this development? Not with confusion or disturbance. He serenely replied,

> Go tell that fox, "I will drive out demons and heal people today and tomorrow, and on the third day I will reach my goal." In any case, I must keep going today and tomorrow and the next day (Luke 13:32, 33).

He knew what He was doing, and all the opposition, all the threats in the world, were not going to deflect Him.

Sometimes even friends got in Jesus' way. On one occasion, Peter did not understand His direction and was obstinately getting in the way. Jesus rebuked him, saying,

> Out of my sight, Satan! You are a stumbling block to me; you do not have in mind the things of God, but the things of men (Matthew 16:23).

Not even His friends could be allowed to deflect Him from His goal.

The day came when He could say to God,

> I have brought you glory on earth by completing the work you gave me to do. And now, Father, glorify me in your presence with the glory I had with you before the world began (John 17:5).

And then the ultimate statement:

> It is finished (John 19:30).

The apostle Paul was also like that. Beat him and leave him for dead, shipwreck him and throw him in the ocean, lock him in prison—and he would hold true to his target (2 Corinthians 11:21-33).

The Christians of the New Testament were like that. They were captivated by the mission Jesus had given them. They knew who they were and why they were here. They lived for their Master's enterprise, they focused their lives upon it, they labored for it, and many of them died for it. It welded those people together and moved them harmoniously in the same direction. No other kind of church will put fire in men's bones. No other kind of church will rally people, inspire them, and challenge them to be the people of God. No other kind of church will strike the spark to inflame the souls of people, to enliven their minds, to call forth their energies into a great movement.

## The Right Kinds of Goals

### Consistent

Effective servants of Christ have that quality of a clear and dominant goal that pulls their energies together and makes them effective instruments in the hands of God. They have a consistent sense of direction that channels everything in life together and moves toward the target. That does not mean such persons never get derailed, but when they do, they simply get back on the track and continue.

This quality may be thought of as single-mindedness, in which life is on one consistent track.

Jesus illustrated this quality in several ways. You can't plow, He said, looking back over your shoulder (Luke 9:62). You have to set your plow and your eye in the same direction and go for it. You can't serve two masters (Matthew 6:24). You've got to decide on a master and serve him wholeheartedly. If God is your master, then serve Him. If another is your master, then don't fool yourself, face up to the fact and serve him consciously. But pick your master and serve him single-mindedly. You can't travel two roads (Matthew 7:13). At the crossroads you have to pick one and go that way.

We must eat, breathe, and sleep the purpose for which we exist. No other servant can be an ultimate success, can be truly faithful in his Master's enterprise.

## Specific

Near where I grew up in southern Indiana, there was a water mill. Inside it the heavy millstones turned, one on the other, to grind the grain into flour and meal. A series of gears linked the stones to the great water wheel outside. Water came down through a millrace and hit the vanes of the wheel at precisely the right place. This gigantic wheel and those enormous stones did not require a Niagara Falls to operate them. A very small stream of water did the job, but every drop of that water was carefully directed to strike the target at exactly the right place.

The same principle applies to the church. Its success requires that all we have be channeled directly on the target, so that energies and resources are not dissipated in many directions. It takes rigorous goal-orientation to gather up all our efforts and channel them to a specific objective. The alternative is to be inert, wandering, or aimless.

Figure 6-1 illustrates this principle in churches. The small circles represent the various components and activities of a congregation: morning worship, Sunday school, youth activities, women's programs, committees, boards, elders, ministers, and the like. In an ineffective congregation these components just spin in their own orbits. They don't go anywhere, even though people stay busy. Efforts are fragmented.

Frankly, this church is far more typical than it should be. Too

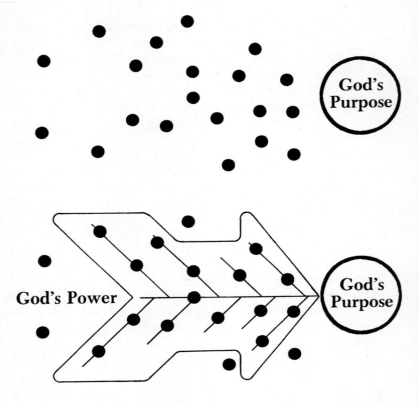

Figure 6-1. *Activities of a congregation or individual, when channeled towards God's purpose*

many churches are made up of many bits and pieces that everyone tries to keep in place but nobody is sure what it is all about.

Figure 6-1 can also represent a minister's life and activity. The circles include hospital calls, attending committee meetings, soothing ruffled feathers, preaching sermons, teaching lessons, counseling people, planning worship services—all the many things that make up ministry in today's congregations. These duties can become a frantic distraction, and ministry like fighting a swarm of bees or groping through a swirling storm of details. Some ministers burn themselves out trying to respond effectively to such scattered demands week after week. Others give up and drift aimlessly through the maze of activities.

That congregation can turn into a very effective one (or that ministry or life can become productive and rewarding) if it is given a direction so that all the components channel together. That is the principle of the millrace: targeting everything so it strikes the goal.

When this is the case, the church is energized and propelled to success by the power of God. One does not see congregations or lives like the first one in Figure 6-1 empowered in this fashion, but those like the one below it do not lack the strength and resources to achieve great accomplishments in God's enterprise. God never fails to bless those who are targeted on His goals and are pulling every effort together to achieve them. That's why some Christians and congregations literally achieve *much more than is humanly possible.* When they and God are in partnership, the impossible suddenly becomes possible. They are fruitful branches and the energy of the Vine courses through them.

## Challenging

About a hundred years ago a railroader approached the minister of a church. His son, he said, had died at age 15. He and his wife would like to do something as a memorial. Could the minister give him some suggestions? The minister thought for a moment and offered an idea. Would they, perhaps, like to provide new carpeting for the church parlor? That was not quite what the man had in mind, and nothing came of the conversation.

Eventually, the railroader did provide a memorial. He was Leland Stanford, Sr.—not only an investor in railroads, but governor of California and, later, United States Senator. The memorial consisted of nine thousand acres of land and twenty-one million dollars to establish the Leland Stanford, Jr. University—now simply known as Stanford University.

Daniel Burnham's injunction is correct:

Make no little plans; they have no magic to stir men's blood.

All productive enterprises are focused on clear, dominant goals. A contemporary writer describes a visit to a successful business corporation. He first talked with the president of the company who, in the course of the conversation, told him precisely the purpose of the institution. The writer was impressed at how clearly and naturally he verbalized it. He talked with other management-level people and found that somewhere in every conversation, each of them stated that same purpose. As he talked with secretaries, they, too, expressed the same clear awareness of the company's purpose. Finally he chatted with a man who was sweeping the floors. He, too, articulated an exact statement of what the institution was striving to accomplish. This successful business enterprise had ingrained in all its people—from the president to the janitor—a strong, clear sense of commitment to its purpose.

The church ought to learn a lesson here. I think we have grossly underestimated people. If we get little response from them, it is probably because we have challenged them to something so puny that they think, "So what?" We have failed to remember that human beings have the capability of being heroic.

In particular, we have made this error with the young. The 15- to 25-year-olds are capable of rising to heroic challenges. When they see that we mean business, many of them will rise to great commitment.

This message comes through loud and clear in Douglas Hyde's *Dedication and Leadership.*[1] Hyde was a ranking official in European Communism for a long time. Eventually he worked his way out of Communist philosophy and looked to the church as its alternative. He was devastated by what he found. He expected to find in the church the same kind of commitment to its cause that the Communists had to theirs, but he did not. He began lecturing churches in an attempt to awaken them. He points out that Communism seriously challenges people to high goals, not just verbally, but in practice. And people buy it! We Christians, he says, have something that ought to challenge people a thousand times more than Communism—if we will start acting toward it the way Communists do about their goals.

## A Norm for Christians

The church described in the New Testament is the standard by which we can measure the church today.

I see disciples and churches in the New Testament who knew exactly what they were here to accomplish. God demonstrated once and for all what He can do with people like that. It is true that they sometimes got off track and wandered temporarily, but the leaders called them back and focused them on the target.

The church described in the New Testament is not abnormal. That is the church being normal. We ought not look back and say, "Oh, those were different times. It's not the same any more." On the contrary, the times are comparable—those and ours. The church is the same (or ought to be). The mission is the same. We can be like them *any time we decide to be.* We dare not brush aside lightly the example that God has given for the church in all ages and in all places. I believe God wants the church always to succeed as it did in those normative days when it was goal-oriented, single-minded, and determined.

I see churches and people falling into two categories. Some are aggressive, others are passive. Some have direction, some are directionless. Some are moving, some just exist. Great churches and great people take God's purposes seriously. They take the Commission to heart. They believe God intends to do not just good things, but great things as He fulfills His purposes through His people.

One minister tried to justify his goalless ministry by using the Parable of the Sower. The sower was not responsible for results, the minister said, only for sowing. After he sowed the seed everywhere, his job was finished.

This is a misuse of the parable. Jesus is talking about the hearts of people who hear the gospel, not about how to farm. No farmer is equally content with scattering precious seed on a footpath or in weed patches where it won't produce. A farmer concentrates on seeding the soil most likely to produce a good harvest. If a farmer farmed the way that preacher apparently carried out his ministry, he would probably go hungry that winter!

We can learn another lesson from the grist mill. Those huge stones must be stopped immediately whenever there is no grain between them, or they will grind each other to bits. If the church is not engaged in doing the work for which it is designed, it had better not go on running or it will destroy itself. I see individual lives and congregations grinding destructively upon themselves because they have lost their focus on God's purpose for them.

## CHAPTER 7

# Strategy-Mindedness

It is one thing to be focused on a goal and another to find the best ways to achieve it. Strategy-mindedness is a matter of intelligently finding those ways and being willing to pay the price, whatever it takes.

I recommend three mottos to every Christian and every church:

(1) *Whatever it takes.* That's the way wars are won. That's the way great reforms are accomplished. That's the way great people and great churches develop.

(2) *Why not?* This question should be used as the challenge whenever negative thinking or small thinking rears its ugly head to discourage bold ventures.

(3) *There is a way—let's find it!* This attitude refuses to admit the impossibility of whatever needs to be undertaken for the success of the enterprise.

## Paul's Example

I wish it were possible to interview Paul. His commitment to the kingdom had some interesting effects on his value system. I would ask, "Paul, tell me, is it better to have money in the bank, a good home, and plenty to eat, or is it better to be broke, hungry, and homeless?"

Most of us would have no trouble answering that question. But I think I know how Paul would respond. "Now that depends," he would doubtless say. "Which one would serve the cause of Christ better? If I can serve Him better through a flourishing life, then fine. But if hardship, deprivation, and hunger would serve Him better, then that's what I would choose."

That is strategy-mindedness. It does not consider which I may prefer, but which is better for the kingdom.

I would ask Paul a second question—"Would you rather be free or in prison?" He would reply, "Well, that depends. If my freedom will serve Christ's mission, then I will protect it and use it to the fullest. But if prison should ever be the more productive option, then so be it."

The time came when prison did, indeed, serve the kingdom better. Some of the richest of the New Testament Scriptures came out of his prison cell; they have been producing for Christ for twenty centuries.

Then I would ask Paul the strangest question yet—"Paul, is it better to live or to die?" Most people would not hesitate an instant in answering that; but again, his answer would be something like, "That depends. Which would accomplish the most for Christ's enterprise? If life, then I'll live. If dying, then bring on the executioner!"

There was a time when Paul was beset by rival preachers proclaiming the gospel not so much to propagate the kingdom, but to distress Paul. But that didn't matter to him. If they were preaching the true gospel and souls were being saved, that was all that mattered. The effect on him was immaterial.

That is strategy-mindedness. The Lord needs many more like Paul.

Strategy-mindedness—that is God's attitude toward His enterprise. It is Paul's attitude. And it is the characteristic needed by all of Christ's people in all times.

## Qualities for Success

A time management dictum says, "Work *smarter,* not *harder.*" I don't think we can make that dichotomy regarding work in

Christ's enterprise. He demands that we work smart *and* hard. Nevertheless, the emphasis on working smart is worth our attention.

Peter Wagner has identified the following qualities among leaders of flourishing, succeeding congregations:

1. Single-minded obedience.
2. Clearly defined objectives.
3. Reliance on discerning research, getting the facts.
4. Ruthlessness in evaluating results. No excuse-making. Are we getting the job done or not? (Wagner advocates *consecrated* pragmatism.)
5. An attitude of optimism and faith, convinced that Christ is building His church and the gates of Hell will not prevail.[1]

Sanctified pragmatism is essential to the kingdom. There is a place for rational effort and planning. Faith has to come out our fingertips before it really accomplishes anything. Congregations ought to do the best planning of which they are capable; they ought to expend the finest efforts they can muster.

Those characteristics not only describe effective Christian leaders, they ought also to be the marks of all Christians and all congregations.

## A Quality Jesus Requires
Jesus speaks often of a certain quality He wants His people to have. To the people of His day, He said,

> When evening comes, you say, "It will be fair weather, for the sky is red," and in the morning, "Today it will be stormy, for the sky is red and overcast." You know how to interpret the appearance of the sky, but you cannot interpret the signs of the times (Matthew 16:2, 3).

I think Jesus is speaking of plain common sense. Why shouldn't we exercise as much common sense about matters of the kingdom as we do in other areas of life? When it comes to the church, why should we turn off our brains and not be as sensible or intelligent as we are about such menial things as the weather?

Nor was Jesus afraid to use figures of speech out of the business world. The Parable of the Talents itself is right out of that context and there is a great deal of common sense in it. It makes good sense that when someone gives you money to invest, he expects you to go out and make as much as you can with it. When God gives us His kingdom enterprise, He expects us to make the most of it. That is common business sense applied to the kingdom.

In Luke 16, another parable deals with this same quality. It is the parable we call "The Unrighteous Steward." The steward manages the affairs of a man of great wealth. Unrighteous is a mild word to apply to him.

He has been mismanaging and robbing the owner. The owner finds out and prepares to fire him. Now the manager is in a panic. How will he live? He is too weak to do manual labor for a living and he is too proud to beg. Then he has a brilliant idea and sets to work juggling the accounts, using the master's money to set himself up for life with his master's many debtors. Jesus said, "The master commended the dishonest manager because he had acted shrewdly. For the people of this world are more shrewd in dealing with their own kind than are the people of the light."

Do not misunderstand—the master does not praise his manager for being a scoundrel, but for being shrewd, for knowing how to get things done. Jesus is not commending the manager's ethics, but his astuteness. Why should the people of the world outthink and outstrip the servants of Christ? The people of the kingdom should approach their task more shrewdly, more intelligently, more strategically than the people of the world approach their tasks.

In another instance, Jesus said we ought to be as shrewd as snakes and as innocent as doves (Matthew 10:16). We ought to be as wise, creative, and resourceful as anyone in the world, but we must operate on the ethics of the kingdom. The kingdom needs bright people who know how to get things done for Christ. Faithfulness, or success, demands it.

One of my favorite authors is A. M. Hunter. In one of his writings he was searching for the precise word to describe the characteristic we are dealing with. He thought perhaps *practical prudence* would describe it, or maybe *shrewdness*. Then Hunter suggested a word that, for me, carries the best meaning of Jesus. He said Jesus wants us to be *savvy*[2]—bright, clever, and creative— knowing how to get things done. That is the way Jesus wants His servants to carry out His enterprise.

Professor Duncan, famed teacher of ministerial candidates at New College in Edinburgh, once said to his students, "What you need, gentlemen, are the three G's—Greek, Grace, and Gumption. If you haven't Greek, you can learn it. If you haven't Grace, you can pray for it. But if you haven't Gumption, the Lord help you!"[3]

Perhaps that is the best word yet to describe this characteristic—gumption. Our Lord needs people with gumption, savvy, shrewdness, prudence; He needs servants who can set His goal before them and say, "We're going to find the way to get it accomplished!"

## Risk-Taking

Productive servants and churches of Christ are willing to take a risk for the sake of success. Faith is a risky business. It moves us out on a limb toward the goal, trusting that through our best wisdom and effort and through God's involvement with us, we will succeed. But we must risk failure in the process.

I know a congregation that has risked heroically and succeeded. As they grew, it became obvious that they would have to construct more facilities. They went into a building program so large that it stretched their resources to the limit, or so it seemed. They were not far into the building program when the leaders became convinced that they should start a new congregation. A number of their families lived across a range of hills in another valley that was rapidly filling with people. Their congregation could not adequately reach that valley, so a new church was needed. In the midst of an already faith-stretching project, they "swarmed" more than one hundred people and started the new church. That was risky. It could have made the difference between managing the new building or collapsing.

As a matter of fact, the hundred people they lost were replaced almost immediately; attendance dipped slightly for a few weeks and then rebounded, larger than ever. With the new building, they have almost doubled in attendance. Now two flourishing congregations serve Christ in that area. The church took a risk for the kingdom's sake, but it was a calculated risk. This must be in the will of God, they reasoned, because that valley must be evangelized. It cannot wait. Their actions may have appeared to jeopardize what they were doing, but they trusted that even the impossible is possible with God.

It is, of course, possible to be foolhardy. That is not the same as faith that dares. But most of us play it far too safe. *We do not undertake what we are sure we could do, even without God's help, let alone what we couldn't do without His help.* Vigorous, effective, growing congregations and individual Christians undertake things they know are beyond human ability; but they do so in the confidence that they and God are in this together. It would, I believe, be better to fail while trying something great for God than to play it safe and never accomplish anything significant.

The decision-making body of one congregation meets around a table with an empty chair at the head. When considering a matter, they never deal with the question of what it will cost until they first discuss to the point of decision whether or not it is needed for the success of God's enterprise. The empty chair, they say, is for their Chairman, who is a billionaire. If it needs to be done, He can find the means.

## Commitment to Excellence

The church has often been beset by sloppy thinking. There is nothing spiritual about stupidity or ineptitude, and there is nothing unspiritual about tough-minded shrewdness and ingenuity in the service of the kingdom. All too much Christian work is undertaken weak-mindedly. God is not glorified by muddle-headedness. He is glorified by servants who use their brains and their brawn in His service.

Somewhere we got the idea that if we just mean well, if we have good intentions and don't deny the faith, then we are being faithful; that this is the measure of success. That idea simply is not true. We can mean well all day long and not produce anything. Jesus says that nothing takes the place of results. We have said, "Well, being sincere is what really counts." No it isn't. Profitability in the enterprise is what counts. If sincerity doesn't get the job done, it is not enough.

We ought to strive for excellence in serving Christ's cause. Earl Nightingale says that the difference between the average person and the excellent person is not usually enormous. The difference is what he calls "the slight edge," just a little more precision, a little more effort, a little more discipline. That is what separates the mediocre from the achiever, the "also ran" from the winner.

A recent chapel speaker at our seminary recounted an incident that had stunned him. He overheard two high school girls, a member and a visitor, talking in the church building. They had attended an event that apparently had been poorly done. The visitor was commenting negatively about it and the church member responded, "Well, what do you expect? After all, it's only a church."

The speaker thought to himself, "My word! Is that the way people think? That sloppy, just-get-it-done-the-easiest-way kind of thinking and effort is all right just because it's the church?" This experience, he said, convinced him that all the work of the church ought to be done the best way possible in order to be productive for the Master.

Elton Trueblood has a way of turning a phrase that makes a point memorable. I heard him quoted recently in this pungent statement: "Holy shoddy is still shoddy."

I fear the church has often said, "Well, its shoddy, but at least it's holy, and that's good enough." Away with this kind of thinking! It will not suffice for the most important enterprise in the world!

## The Church Growth Emphasis

The Church Growth movement is flourishing around the world. It holds bright hope for greater accomplishment in the Lord's enterprise. It deals with two basic concerns:

(1) What is the goal? What is it our Lord wants us to accomplish above everything else?
(2) How can we achieve that goal to the greatest degree?

People in this movement are researching the task to help Christ's servants find the most productive strategies to accomplish His mission in their particular settings. They appeal for us to put our best thinking to work in the service of Jesus, to use all the resources at our disposal and all the determination we can muster. The literature of the movement is high priority reading for Christians in our generation.

How are we to disciple all peoples? Paul wrote, "I have become all things to all men so that by all possible means I might save some" (1 Corinthians 9:22). For us, that may mean, "To the ghetto dweller, I become a ghetto dweller." Rather than trying first to suburbanize these people and make them like us and then bring them to discipleship, we must take Christ to them on their own turf. Rather than pulling them out to our "nice suburban church," we may have to go where they are and build congregations there, in those circumstances. Strategy must prevail in such decisions and plans.

Donald McGavran, founder of the "church growth" way of thinking, has provided an illustration that will help show us how we will know when the work of our congregations is right.

> An automobile is supposed to get one from point A to point B at 55 miles per hour with fair comfort, performance, and economy. Suppose your car is not running well—going only ten miles per hour, pouring black smoke out the back, running rough, and guzzling gasoline. You know the car is not right because it isn't doing what a car is supposed to do. So you take it to a mechanic and say, "Fix it." In the evening you go back and pay the bill. You head for home but the car has the same problems. You return to the shop and tell the mechanic that it is not fixed. He replies, "Oh, it must be. I had my two best men spend the whole day cleaning the upholstery."
>
> That is not strategy-mindedness. You know the car is fixed when it will run 55 miles per hour, does not smoke, and runs smoothly. So you say, "It is not fixed yet." But a day later, he gives you the same story. This time the mechanic says it is fixed because his men gave it a first-class wax job. [4]

What are the lessons of the illustration? First, until you have a goal, you don't have a criterion to know when things are right. You will know by its growth when the church is doing things right. Is the kingdom growing because of its work or not?

Second, your criterion indicates what kinds of things you must work on. In the case of the car, you don't work on upholstery and wax jobs to get it running right. You have to work on such things as carburetion, timing, and spark plugs.

How do you know when your personal life is properly tuned up? When certain things start happening to bring success to Christ's enterprise. How will you know when your church is properly tuned? When the right results are forthcoming. Strategy-mindedness is a matter of finding and using means that produce the right end result.

Form follows function. That is, the thing you are trying to accomplish determines the form to use to accomplish it. I don't think that God, in creation, doodled around in the dust, ended up with the human hand, and said, "I like it. I wonder what it might be good for." No, He had a function for people to fulfill and that function required that people be designed with the hand. The form of the hand was directed by the function it was to perform.

Successful entrepreneurs focus on their goals and creatively find ways to achieve them. Yet in many churches we substitute mindless habit or tradition for forms that function. The kingdom calls for tough-minded servants.

## Strategy-Mindedness and Priorities

Strategy-mindedness requires that we have a clear sense of priorities. Look at Figure 7-1. If that large circle is your goal and the arrows are various means to achieve the goal, which means is best? In this case, one way is as good as another—any of the means reaches the goal.

Now look at Figure 7-2. When the goal is sharpened to a bullseye, which means is best? Obviously, the arrow in the middle. But you cannot know that until you know precisely what it is you are trying to accomplish.

When the church has a broad, general sense of purpose, it is hard to determine, among many "good" things, what the priorities are.

In missionary work, many "good" things often need to be done: medical aid, education, providing food and clothing, agricultural assistance, and the like. When one veteran missionary began to evaluate his work, he discovered that many good things had been done. Lifetimes had been invested. Much money had been spent. But in terms of building the kingdom, little had been accomplished. When the missionary began to think this way, he did not cease all his other mission activities. He sharpened his focus on the one thing he was really there to do, building the kingdom by

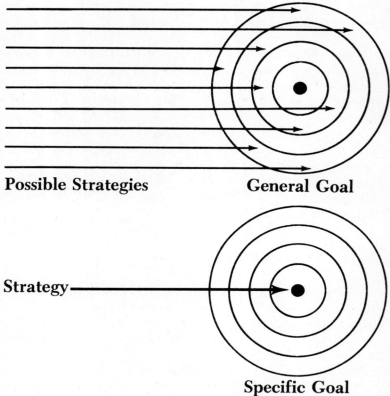

**Possible Strategies**  **General Goal**

**Strategy**  **Specific Goal**

Figure 7-1. *How specific goals help define strategy*

*making disciples.* Then all the other activities began to find their proper places as strategies or means for accomplishing the central priority. When the priorities were put in working order, the whole mission functioned productively.

We must stringently evaluate what we are doing in terms of its contribution to our purpose for being here. If it does not contribute, we may not have time for it.

Look back at Figure 6-1. When the arrow was drawn around the dots representing church activities, some of the dots fell outside. These are activities or procedures which, when the church evaluates them, are found not to be productive of the goal. A wise church may well decide it does not have time for them and redirect its energies and resources to other endeavors.

Donald McGavran has observed that many Christian workers build whole theologies to justify lack of disciple-making. (It is assumed they do this unconsciously, not deliberately.) These theologies focus on *searching* for the "lost sheep" rather than *finding* them and bringing them into the fold. They focus on *sowing* rather than *harvesting*. They focus on *proclaiming* the gospel rather than *persuading* people to become followers of Jesus.

Evangelism is the ultimate center, the bulls-eye. These questions remain: Are we finding and bringing in the lost sheep? Are we harvesting and conserving the grain? Are we persuading more and more people to become disciples of Jesus and responsible members of His body, the church?

## Summary

A strategy-minded person seeks the best ways of fulfilling the Lord's purpose and is willing to do whatever it takes. Such a person has a quality of shrewdness, savvy, or gumption, which he uses to achieve his Lord's ends. Nor is such a person afraid to take risks, aim for high goals, or constantly evaluate the means that are currently being used.

---

[1]C. Peter Wagner, *Your Church Can Grow* (Glendale CA: Regal, 1976), pp. 30-32.

[2]A. M. Hunter, *Interpreting the Parables* (Naperville, IL: SCM Book Club, 1960), p. 67.

[3]Cited by Hunter, op. cit., p. 67.

[4]Donald McGavran, in an address to the faculty of Cincinnati Christian Seminary.

# CHAPTER 8

# Effective Congregations

## A Complex Balance

The key to productivity and growth of churches has been elusive. Success is a complex matter seldom produced by just one cause. Nearly always, it is the result of many interacting factors.

Churches must deal with concerns about what they believe and teach—*doctrine*. They must also give attention to developing the right practices, including effective preaching and teaching, fellowship, friendliness, and methods of equipping and mobilizing the members—*function*. And they must work with the tangible and measurable concerns such as buildings, equipment, local environment, and organization—*empirical factors*.

The functional and empirical factors deal with the pragmatic concerns that are under our control and are to be managed for the best results in the kingdom enterprise.

Figure 8-1 shows how these three elements—doctrine, function, and empirical factors—interact to produce effectiveness. All are essential to God's enterprise. If any of them is not properly operating, growth is unlikely, and if it does occur, its validity is questionable.

Let's look at some individual elements of church life and see how they contribute to the success of God's enterprise.

## Time and Place

*Church #1* is in a rapidly growing area. Houses cannot be built fast enough to meet the demand. Property values soar. The church is also skyrocketing in growth. It is making great strides in the spiritual development of its people as well as growth in numbers. All elements of the Great Commission are being achieved to a high degree.

Surely this congregation is succeeding in the enterprise the Master has entrusted to them. They are being faithful to their trust. Many people look at that congregation with the attitude, "Certainly they are succeeding. We could, too, if we had their location and all its advantages." But within two miles of that church's building is Church #2.

*Church #2* is in that same fruitful place, but it is withering. When people excuse their lack of achievement by saying, "If we were just in the right place, we could do great things," they must admit the existence of churches like this one.

*Church #3* meets in a white frame building beside a country road. While it continues to exist, not much is going on. Once in a while, they baptize one of their children who grows to the age of response, but beyond that they are not reaching anyone. People are moving away and the congregation is slowly shrinking. They hold the usual meetings and make an attempt to study the Bible, but there is little evidence that spiritual growth is doing any better than numerical growth. "Well, that's understandable," the people say. "What can we expect under these circumstances?" That verdict sounds reasonable, except for the example of Church #4.

*Church #4* is in the same kind of location. Yet this congregation is growing spiritually and reaches a surprising number of new people—even in this unpromising place! Several building programs have added space for growth. The congregation is well equipped and organized. People from a number of nearby towns have been won through their efforts.

Like John the Baptist, they are out in the wilderness, but God's work is going on, and the whole countryside has come flocking.

It is hard to prove that being at the right place at the right time is, alone, the key to success for congregations. McGavran says that if conditions are handled properly, a church can probably grow anywhere—with the possible exception of Antarctica!

## Correct Doctrine

Some people will insist that correct doctrine is the key to growth and vitality. Yet some churches with very sound doctrine stagnate while others with unsound doctrine flourish. The four churches described above are equally sound in doctrine. If one asks the minister of a growing church why they are growing, he is likely to say, "Because we preach the gospel." And if you ask the preacher of a non-growing church why they do not grow, *he* is likely to say, "Because we preach the gospel"!

If a church excels in the functional and empirical areas, it may grow even if it has serious problems in the doctrinal area. In that case it grows in spite of its doctrine, not because of it.

But real problems arise when another congregation tries to use that church as a model for success. If a church leader looks at a congregation he considers successful, and they happen to have a different view of some doctrine, he might draw a false conclusion that the "success" is caused by that difference. He may be more doctrinally correct than the church he is looking at, but he assumes they are correct and he is wrong because they are "succeeding." And he assumes that if he adopts their doctrine, he, too, will succeed.

For a congregation to be effective it has to be doctrinally sound, but that alone won't assure success. Churches seldom grow if they seal off the doctrinal sector and focus on it alone. They tend to become pharisaical, sour, and legalistic. They usually lack qualitative as well as quantitative achievement.

## A Secret of Programming

People commonly assume that success is the result of some kind of program. The successful church must have found some secret of organization or polity. And so some churches scour the country for the latest "program" or "module" that they can "plug into" their situation and have automatic success. But such ready-made solutions usually do not work.

It is said that Alexander Campbell, influential Christian leader in the early nineteenth century, owned a farm, published a journal, carried a gold-headed walking stick, and preached for two hours with his hands folded on top of his walking stick. And a whole generation of preachers bought farms, published journals,

72

carried gold-headed walking sticks, and preached two-hour sermons. But it did not make Alexander Campbells of them! These traits were not the source of his real power. The other preachers were copying the wrong things. What they should have copied was his fervent motivation and his commitment to study.

Effective programs are always homemade, hammered out with prayer and wisdom for the particular situation. Try to plug them in somewhere else and they don't usually work. Still, many churches go from program to program with little result.

What churches must do is identify the underlying principles that cause programs in another church to work, and then develop their own programs to implement those principles in their own unique way.

## Supernatural Variation

Some people attribute success in a church to some supernatural variation. "God is really blessing them," is the explanation frequently offered. Granting the fact of God's blessing, the question remains, "Does God arbitrarily decide to bless one church and not another?"

One might suspect that crediting God alone with success (or the lack of it) may be an easy rationalization to shift responsibility.

## The Spiritual Dimension

Look again at Figure 8-1. It is possible for a church to focus on the surface dimension of the doctrinal, functional, and empirical aspects in such a way that they are trusting human cleverness, human dynamics, human effort, and human organization. They become a "secular congregation" without spiritual depth. If they succeed, they do so in the same way any human organization does.

Even doctrine can be handled humanistically. The Pharisees and Sadducees were great experts on points of doctrine. They argued theology the way Greek philosophers argued philosophy. It is possible to concentrate intently on doctrine and still be a secular congregation. It is also possible to handle the functional and empirical factors on a purely human organizational level.

For a congregation truly to succeed, they must have the third

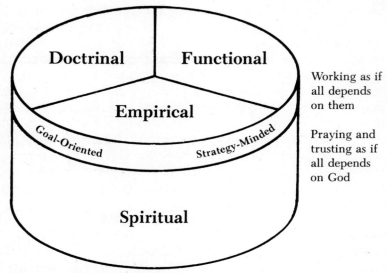

Figure 8-1. *Effective churches*

dimension--the indwelling God who produces His results through them. They must truly operate on the promise that with God nothing is impossible. If a congregation commits itself to those things to which God is committed, He will surely enable them to do it, so that even the impossible becomes possible.

However, if a congregation focuses on the spiritual dimension alone, ignoring the others, they engage in pious presumption. They forfeit their responsible role as partners with God.

It is tragic that spiritually sincere people pray and believe in God but do not know how to bring to the partnership those strategic plans and efforts that make for greater achievement. They never fully bring to God the goal-orientation and strategy-mindedness for which He waits. The church falls far short of their potential when, all the while, their insights, knowledge, skills, and hard work could have made all the difference.

Figure 8-1 also includes two other qualities. These pull all the other factors together into an integrated whole. They are goal-orientation and strategy-mindedness.

The result is a church in which people work as if everything depended on them and pray and trust God as if everything depended on Him. Such a church is productive of God's goals.

# Use of Resources

The church does not "have its act together" until it gives balanced attention to all the elements described above. Even the most practical concerns in the empirical sector (buildings, equipment, etc.) need not be thought of as unspiritual. These concerns are part of the strategy-mindedness that Jesus advocates for His servants.

In my own ministry, I focused only on the doctrinal, functional, and spiritual elements for a long time. But I found that these practical matters also influenced the degree to which the church achieved its potential. Through an educational program, I discovered that much research has been done on these practical institutional matters. Today this research is available to the church. We do not have to work by trial and error as much as we once did.

Theories and research in such fields as leadership, administration, management, sociology, psychology, and anthropology provide insights to help us act more intelligently as partners with God. Let's glean every morsel of this knowledge that can be useful to the kingdom and bring it to God's service!

Alexander Campbell was a good example. Here was a brilliant and learned man who brought into the service of the gospel the resources of philosophy, language, logic, and many other disciplines. At the same time, he built his study with the windows only in the roof to remind himself always of his need for "light from above." He linked the resources of man with the power of God in such a way that he accomplished magnificent things.

The Church Growth movement has given serious attention to this task. One stream of it has studied the effect of such practical factors as the examples that follow:

## Two Examples

1. *Adding new groups.* New groups like Sunday-school classes, study groups, and service units provide the dynamic vacuum that will draw and hold new people.

One congregation I visited had been doing many things right and were growing well, but then they quit growing, and they couldn't understand it.

It took only a moment to illustrate why. Three years before, the church was averaging 147 in attendance. In the past three years they had added six new classes. The previous Sunday there had been 50 people in those six classes. That 50, added to the previous average, totaled 197. Their actual attendance was 202, within five of what could have been predicted by the adding of the classes. To continue growing, they would have to add more classes, either by building new classrooms or going to double sessions.

If a church wants to grow, it must provide for growth in such common sense matters as more classrooms or worship space, more leaders to take care of more people, and adequate (actually, surplus) parking space. When your capacity is full, you can't go on growing.

2. *Flexibility in leadership.* As a church grows, it requires more leaders. A church can grow no larger than the number of people it is organized to care for. Leaders must represent the newer people and not be restricted only to the "old guard." The style of decision-making must adapt.

As a church grows, policy-making must centralize while administrative decisions and implementation must decentralize. A church will plateau at a certain size if every detail must pass through a central board. It simply can't outgrow such a structure.

As a church grows, the preacher's role must adjust. He can personally pastor only so many people, beyond that he must begin ministering through others. Involving more unsalaried members in ministry and addition of staff members is a basic necessity if churches are to continue growing. Lyle Schaller, one of the best informed student of churches today, says that one minister can manage a congregation averaging 200 or less in attendance. A church must add one staff member for every 100 additional people in attendance. Even at that, a church is staffed only for maintenance.[1]

## Limitations

Church leaders ought to take a second and third look before they decide that their environment limits their growth. I consulted with a congregation recently regarding their future planning. They perceived their field as limited—a small community with

76

many churches. Practically everyone was accounted for, they assumed. Their mental images about their future potential were formed accordingly. They were running about 200 in attendance and assumed only slight growth could be projected.

Prior to my visit I asked them to secure county population figures and to poll every church to see how many people were accounted for. They found a county population of 30,000 (far larger than the size of the town had led them to assume). All the churches together accounted for only 8,000 people (far fewer than they expected). That left 22,000 people effectively unreached in their immediate field. If they were to set goals of reaching only ten percent of that number, they would have to think in terms of a congregation of 2,000!

The best way for a congregation to fulfill Christ's mandate is a very individual matter. A large, goal-oriented, strategy-minded church in a small community seeks to grow qualitatively and seriously evangelizes its community, but there are severe limitations to its evangelistic potential. Non-Christians are a minority, and most of them have been approached repeatedly with the gospel. The church continues to reach some of them and the children of member families. But the field is not highly fruitful.

This congregation has chosen to express its commitment through involvement in missionary activities away from home. It gives more to missions than it spends at home. It is in close communication with its missionaries, praying for them and sending members to assist them for short periods of time. That is their best expression of faithful productivity for the kingdom.

Another goal-oriented, strategy-minded church is led by an outstanding preacher and a large and capable staff. The local work flourishes. The preacher is also gifted in his ability to hold meetings in other churches to help them rise to new heights of effectiveness. Consequently, he spends a great deal of his time away from home during the week. The congregation encourages him. "When he is out helping other churches do their job better," they say, "that's part of this congregation's ministry. He extends our work far and wide."

Each congregation must face its mission realistically, with a strong commitment to Christ's mandate and strategic decision-making.

# Summary

The key to a successful church does not involve one single aspect of church life, but a complex balance of several: doctrinal, functional, and empirical matters, plus a solid dependence upon God through faith. All these factors are tied together by commitment to God's objectives and by a strategy-minded pursuit of those goals.

---

[1] Although Schaller deals with this subject in a number of books, see, for example, *Growing Plans* (Nashville: Abingdon Press, 1983), p. 115. Schaller's voluminous writings are "must" readings for church leaders.

# CHAPTER 9

# Competent Leadership

No current issue is more critical than that of leadership. Today's static conditions in churches can be attributed, more than any other single factor, to inadequate implementation of Biblical ideals for leadership.

What must the leadership become if churches are to fulfill their reason for existence as fully and rapidly as possible?

## A Biblical Structure for Dynamic Christian Leadership

### Responsible Christians

The basic unit of responsibility and function must be the individual Christian. He is the structural cell of which the body of Christ consists. Here resides that functioning life which, under the energizing headship of Christ and effectively set in order by leadership, causes the body to grow and build itself up in love "as each part does its work" (Ephesians 4:16).

Every Christian must see himself as Christ's agent, responsible in his personal life and in terms of his role in his local congregation. All Christians must focus their lives around the commitment to bring Christ's mission to success. It is leadership's role to bring the people to such maturity and mobilize them into a truly vigorous body.

R. E. O. White captures the essence of the qualities Jesus desires in His people:

> Himself vigorous in challenge, controversy, action, Jesus loved energetic people—the "sons of thunder", impulsive Peter, the fearless Baptist, wholehearted Paul, the importunate widow, the efficient bridesmaids, the midnight hammerer, the far sighted rascal, the enthusiast who sold all, the "violent" storming the kingdom, sinners who "press" into heaven. Contrast His strictures upon those who (as in Noah's day) eat and drink and drift, who wait for results they should work for, who *say* much but do nothing. For Him, faith was anything but lazy-mindedness![1]

But such vigorous qualities seem to be woefully lacking among many individual Christians today, as may be seen in the following conditions:

- The frequent burnout of the few who carry more than their share of responsibility while others are idle.
- The low level of available time, energy, and resources in comparison to the potential and the need.
- The diverting inward of existing concern, time, energy, and resources that could and should be channeled outward to expansion.
- "Peter Pan" Christians who refuse to grow up to mature competence, remaining infants to be cared for by the church when they should become contributors to the success of the cause (see Hebrews 5:12ff).
- The cultural redefinition of discipleship into churchmanship, with persons going onto membership lists more as patrons or clients of the church (which becomes a religious service institution) than soldiers in the task force of Christ in the world.
- The typical American habit of delegating responsibility upward to corporate abstractions rather than shouldering responsibilities as individuals.
- Church leaders who keep their people as dependent children rather than equipping them for ministry and setting them free to function.

- Failure to disciple the peoples of the world in this generation—
so far.

The Protestant reformation made strides in restoring the Biblical concept of the priesthood of all believers. But this correction went only halfway. Christians realized that they have access to God through Christ without other human intermediaries, but they failed to realize that priesthood is also a matter of service or ministry. If all Christians are priests, they have the responsibility to function as God's ministers.

The restoration movement attacked the same issue from the standpoint of the clergy-laity dichotomy. The early leaders of the movement saw the "hireling" character of the clergy as an evil to be corrected. Their intention was to recognize all Christians as "ministers," but the actual (and unintentional) result effectively hobbled churches and leaders by making all Christians "laymen."

## Functioning Leaders

The church, under the headship of Christ, is to be set in order (structured, made functional or operational, equipped, mobilized) by its leaders (Ephesians 4:7ff). Leadership is the function that fosters and maintains the church's focus on its divine purpose, promotes intelligent efforts to achieve it, and keeps counterproductive processes in abeyance.

Leadership operates between two poles: the people on one hand, and their goals on the other. It is the function of helping that body of people move toward achieving their goals. Whoever does this is a leader. *Whoever does not do this is not a leader, no matter what title he may wear.*

When progress is being made or success achieved, somebody is causing it. Inertia can just happen, but not movement—it is *caused.* When a church is alive, effective, and progressing, somebody is emphasizing, clarifying, and reminding people of their purpose; somebody is keeping objectives in the spotlight; somebody is showing people how to merge their efforts to accomplish their common goals; somebody is challenging and inspiring them. In other words, somebody is leading.

Douglas Hyde attributes the success of Communist leaders to "their ability to fire the imagination, create a sense of dedication and send their followers into effective, meaningful action."[2] Leadership is, by nature, dynamic. It is a function, rather than simply a title or an office. Unfortunately, offices are sometimes held by nonleaders or antileaders; and the result is inertia, if not disorder.

Depending on whether the leadership function is operating, churches may be dynamic or static. The leadership of dynamic and static churches can be contrasted as follows:

| | |
|---|---|
| *Leaders* spark the achievement of goals, acting as "accelerators," causing the right things to happen. | *Office holders* act as "brakes," controlling, restraining, containing, maintaining the status quo. |
| They are concerned about enabling and equipping the saints. | They are concerned about power, authority, "checks and balances." |
| They are at the head of the movement, causing it to happen. | They are dragged along by any movement that may occur. Like rocks in a stream, any accomplishments must flow around them. |

### Dynamic Churches

Figure 9-1 describes the dynamics of churches on two axes. The horizontal axis ranges from passive on the left to active on the right. All churches will fall somewhere along this dimension and so will individuals. The vertical axis describes the focus of commitments, priorities, or objectives. This focus is often a "hidden agenda" held by individuals or churches rather than an "official" set of goals. To determine where commitments, priorities, or objectives really lie, we may have to look not at what we *say*, but at the way we *behave*. A hidden agenda may also be hidden even from the person who holds it. If you want to know the primary commitment of a Christian, for example, look at how he spends his time, where he expends his energies, what he does with his money. If you want to know the focus of a congregation, do not look at its official statements, but at its board actions, budgets, and programs.

| | Passive | Commitments Priorities Objectives | Active | |
|---|---|---|---|---|
| Bureaucratic Inertia | Commitment in name only. Clichés espoused but inert. | **Kingdom's Enterprise** | Success of the enterprise as the end toward which all else is directed. Bold, hard, faith-filled planning, decisions, and effort. | Faithfulness |
| | Issues of "ivory tower" variety. Intellectual ping-pong among theoreticians. | **Ideological Concerns** | Bigotry, militancy over issues for their own sake. Pharisaism, propagandizing, legalism, controversy, name-calling. | Chauvinism |
| | Maintenance of bureaucratic routine; rigidity; rules above rationality. | **Institutional Concerns** | Institution's success is "hidden agenda" to which all else is subservient. Promotionalism, competition. | Private Empire-Building |
| | Maintenance of bureaucratic routine. Defensiveness toward other departments. Rules above rationality. | **Departmental Concerns** | Department's success is "hidden agenda" to which all else is subservient. "Politicking," maneuvering for advantage. | |
| | Convenience is the norm. Rules privately applied above rationality. | **Personal Concerns** | Personal success, ambition, needs as "hidden agenda" to which all else is subservient. "Politicking," maneuvering for power, advantage. | |

Figure 9-1. *Levels of commitment in a congregation.* The vertical axis shows the different levels of commitment, with the most destructive level, Personal Concerns, at the bottom, and the most constructive level, the Kingdom's Enterprise, at the top. The horizontal axis describes both the passive (left) and active (right) expressions of these concerns.

The lowest level on the vertical axis is self-centered commitment by the individual Christians. Here, passive people may seek only to have their convenient routine undisturbed, maintaining the status quo despite the mandates of goal-orientation and strategy-mindedness. At this level, active individuals may seek personal goals, using the church to succeed in meeting some private need or ambition. Their behaviors include demanding attention or maneuvering for position, power, or prestige. This dynamic may be blatantly obvious or subtle and difficult to identify.

Either direction at this level, to the right or left, sidetracks the success of God's enterprise. The level of concern can be easily blocked at this level unless we are constantly alert. Commitment must flow all the way to the top, at which the success of the enterprise is actively sought, and it must neither be sidetracked nor blocked.

At the next level up, commitment is to some department or activity of the church such as a board or committee, youth program, music function, or women's organization. Again, at this level, bureaucratic inertia may resist the kinds of changes necessary if the church is to become more productive. Ralph Neighbour's title for his little book speaks volumes regarding this problem: *The Seven Last Words of the Church: We Never Did It That Way Before.*[3] Or these departments may focus so actively upon their provincial goals through vigorous campaigning, raising unrest, "politicking," or maneuvering for advantage, that the higher commitments of the church suffer. Again, either branch is a sidetrack to pursuit of the mandated enterprise.

At the next level, the entire church, in its institutional nature, is the focal point of commitment. This may express itself in passive resistance to progress even when rationality in terms of kingdom success demands it. Or the church may so actively seek institutional goals that kingdom concerns are displaced. Promotionalism, intercongregational rivalry, and obsession with institutional concerns are symptoms of this problem. Another sidetrack! I have dealt more fully with these dynamics in my book, *The Church On Purpose.*[4]

The next level deals with ideological concerns, matters of doctrine or philosophy. People may focus on these passively, only theoretically espousing them to little effect. People may spend hours playing intellectual games with all sorts of theological issues. Library shelves are filled with the results of lifetimes spent in such pursuits. This becomes a sidetrack when such efforts never actually cause movement and mandated results in the kingdom's enterprise suffer. Even "good" theology may become a hindrance to the kingdom when it becomes its own end. Theology must deliberately contribute to the goal or it becomes a sidetrack or a blockage.

Active people may militantly propagandize for this or that issue, some of which may truly be crucial to Biblical Christianity. But this becomes a problem, a sidetrack, when obsession with the issue becomes an end in itself, rather than a means for advancing the kingdom of God. Persons in this category may make little contribution to the enterprise of God, despite all the heat and smoke they generate. And, tragically, their tactics may be disastrously counterproductive to the enterprise. Might it be that some militant "defenders of the faith," who are actually correct in their positions, may still be found "unfaithful" as defined by Jesus in the Parable of the Talents? I am aware that I run the danger of being misunderstood at this point. I would not for a moment imply that ideological concerns are not important, even imperative! Standing for the truth must never be compromised—but such a stance must be consciously, deliberately, directed toward productiveness in Christ's mandate. Otherwise, it may become a counterproductive sidetrack that captures and imprisons minds and energies.

Ultimately, kingdom concerns must occupy the highest level of commitment for the congregation and individual Christians. The touchstone for every thought, decision, action, or program at every level must be the question, "Is this helping the kingdom grow?" Productivity in the Master's objectives must be tangible, measurable, provable! It is insufficient to hold such commitments in name only; they must actively promote the success of God's enterprise as the priority above all other concerns.

Commitment must flow upward through all levels to the highest kingdom-level concerns. All other concerns must be subservient to these. When the flow is to the left at any level, the church stagnates in inertia. When the flow is to the right at any level other than kingdom concerns, diversion or fragmentation occurs. When the flow is downward, the congregation is progressively retarded. And when private personal concerns are the focal point, a church degenerates into a free-for-all where individuals compete for their own ends.

Yet another observation may be drawn from the paradigm with application for other Christian organizations such as colleges, missionary groups, evangelistic associations, publishers, and the like. The wisest public relations strategy for such an organization is not to focus on the institution and its needs directly but upon God's enterprise and how the institution is helping to achieve it. I believe the day is nearly over when Christian people will support unproductive institutions for their own sakes or out of emotional attachment. And I take this to be a positive symptom of maturity among Christians. If I am correct, the worst thing an institution can do will be to focus attention on itself, its private goals, or even its own survival.

## Competence in Leadership

I lived for a few years on the West Coast and enjoyed watching people surfing. I saw in it an illustration of ministry. When a wave came along, some would-be surfers would tackle it. Many were awkward and ungainly; most of them would "wipe out." I see some ministers doing that—attacking the dynamics of ministry and really trying but lacking the mastery of it. It is one thing for surfers to wipe out. It is an infinitely more tragic thing for a man's life of serving the kingdom to wipe out.

Other surfers could stay on the board and ride the wave to shore with poise, balance, and surely a great sense of fulfillment. It is a magnificent achievement to watch. I see some ministers doing that, too—attacking those same dynamics of ministry but with a mastery that achieves much for the kingdom and provides fulfillment for the minister himself.

There are few "born surfers." Surfers who attain mastery are those who have learned to do the right things. The most competent of them study surfing, a very sophisticated body of knowledge based on hydraulics, physics, mechanics, oceanology, physiology, and psychology. Surfers have to work at their craft, too, but with that body of information, they can work at it intelligently.

A few people seem to have been "born" to the ministry, but the rest of us must learn or fail. Some attack the task on a trial and error basis; of these, a few make it, and many do not. Others, however, find ways to learn about those things that make up ministry; they go at ministry *intentionally*. Like expert surfers, they inform themselves and approach the task with knowledge, design, and deliberation, as well as experience. Most men in this category not only become producers for the kingdom but they find their work personally fulfilling. Most of them are also lifelong learners. They study their art as long as they live, ever refining and ever growing.

One experienced minister of Christian education told of finding the perfect resource for his ministry. It had, he said, the information he had been seeking for years—the answer to many of his needs were there. Ironically, that resource was a notebook, in his own handwriting, from a college class he did not remember ever taking! At age twenty he did not recognize the relevance of the material, and it went in one ear, into the notebook, and into a file. After years of experience the information took on an entirely new relevance to him.

That is one reason education must be lifelong. It must keep cycling back to meet the ever-emerging times of readiness to learn. Some of my most rewarding work is done in specially scheduled seminars for full-time ministers. These men have been in the ministry for five, fifteen, as many as forty years. They seize and apply insights and report progress in their work with such a zest that makes it a joy to work with them.

## Components of Competence

Figure 9-2 conceptualizes competence in a leader the same way Figure 8-1 in the previous chapter conceptualized competence in churches. Competence is composed of several functions.

*Knowledge.* The upper left quadrant of the circle represents the kind of things a person must know in order to lead the church well. The most important knowledge is knowledge of the Scripture, but knowledge in many other fields can also serve the kingdom well.

*Functional Skills.* The lower left quadrant represents those skills

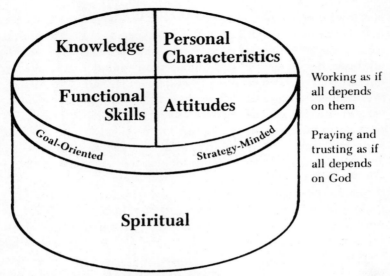

Figure 9-2. *Competent Christian leaders*

and abilities necessary to the practice of Christian leadership. These may be thought of as functional requisites—what a person must be able to do in order to serve the Master's enterprise well.

*Attitudes and Personal Characteristics.* Competence in leadership, however, also requires the proper motivation, attitudes, and commitments. And it demands qualities in an individual's personal life that are consistent with Christian ideals. These are indicated in the two right quadrants of the diagram.

In all these areas, the finest wealth of resources in all history are available to Christian leaders, both through print and other media as well as through a rich variety of learning events. I urge leaders to strive to stay abreast of the aids available in such areas as preaching, teaching, communications, leadership, administration, counseling, personal life and relationships, and family life.

## The Spiritual Dimension

These matters can be approached humanistically, as one might approach any profession. I used to know a man who was a minister of a church in a major denomination. He was a professional in this sense. He confessed to me one day that he did not believe the precepts of the Bible and Christianity but was in the ministry because he preferred it to any other profession. It provided the lifestyle he liked, a comfortable income, a freedom of schedule. He had the knowledge and skills of practice and had put together a professional approach to ministry. As far as his own goals were concerned, he was succeeding.

All these other qualities must have the undergirding depth of the spiritual life, and the whole must be integrated by the qualities of goal-orientation and strategy-mindedness, if ultimate and legitimate productivity is to be achieved.

## Integration

Some people make the naive assumption that a proper spiritual life will take care of everything. There is no need, they say, to think about other matters; God will take care of everything.

This attitude borders on impertinence. A person who is going to serve Christ ought to bring to Him the best that he can learn and develop. He ought to provide all he can and, at the same time, trust God to make up what is still lacking. I do not know why we should expect God to do for us what we could be doing for ourselves. If the secular workplace will not tolerate sloppy, haphazard performance on the part of its people, why should God have to put up with less than the best?

The competent leader learns to understand his attitudes, values, motivations, and commitments and to bring them in line with God's will. He works on those skills, abilities, and details of action and conduct that will make him a vessel of excellence that Christ can use magnificently. He is constantly enriching his knowledge. He gives careful attention to the way he conducts his personal life. He does not trust in these matters alone to make himself an effective instrument in God's service but he offers them to God to be used of Him. He works in partnership with God to accomplish as much as possible in His enterprise, and as he does so, the Master considers him successful and faithful as His servants.

Many Christians measure up well, and would be considered successes by the Master. But I am concerned by the degree of shoddy work and foggy thinking that can be observed among Christ's servants. It is no glory to Christ for one of His people to be undisciplined in habit and attitude, to muddle through and expect the Lord to accomplish things in spite of him.

89

I appeal for an appropriate attitude of professionalism in Christian leaders. Not that these people ought to trust in human elements, but that they bring to Christ the most disciplined life, the best utilized potential, the most highly developed abilities, and the best ordered life, with time managed and mind under control.

It is inexcusable not to pray as fervently as we can, work as hard as we can, think with all the intelligence we have, give attention to the characteristics of our personal and family lives that add effectiveness to Christian leadership. These are the ideals Paul sets forth in the letters to Timothy and Titus regarding their own servanthood and that which they seek to develop in others.

I live by the conviction that it is possible for the life of Christian leadership to be not only productive, but also satisfying, even exuberant! I am convinced that it ought to be so and that it is possible to develop the competence to make it so.

## Summary

The work of a leader is to help the church move toward achieving its goals. Leadership is a function, not a title or office. To be most effective, leaders must integrate their knowledge, skills, and personal qualities and attitudes with a deep and sustaining spiritual life.

Truly successful leaders are also lifelong learners. There has never before been such a vast array of resources available for the minister who wishes to improve his leadership qualities.

---

[1] R. E. O. White, *Five Minutes with the Master* (Grand Rapids: William B. Eerdmans Publishing Company, 1965), p. 242.

[2] Douglas Hyde, *Dedication and Leadership;* (Notre Dame, IN: University of Notre Dame Press, 1966).

[3] Ralph Neighbour, *The Seven Last Words of the Church: We Never Did It That Way Before.* (Grand Rapids, MI: Zondervan Publishing House), 1973.

[4] Joe S. Ellis, *The Church On Purpose.* (Cincinnati: Standard Publishing, 1982), pp. 100-104.

# Implementation

CHAPTER 10

# The Restoration Movement

Early in the nineteenth century, people began to dream of the church brought to its highest fulfillment. The restoration movement was born of a vision of a church restored in essential faith and practice, unified, and winning the world to Christ.

## A Historical View

### Its Principles

At its beginning, the leaders of the restoration movement worked according to the following principles:

1. Our world is not being brought to discipleship to an effective degree.
2. It must be.
3. If that is to happen, there must come sufficient unity among the people of God that the world perceives Christianity as consistent, proclaiming its central message with one unwavering voice.
4. The existing fragmentation of the church is an intolerable condition and a stumbling block to evangelism. The Great Commission languishes when the world sees Christianity as a confusion of claims and counter-claims. How can they know what Christianity is if we can't even make up our own minds?

5. We can arrive at unity by subjecting all our preferences, prejudices, and traditions to Scripture. In the essentials we will speak with one voice; in everything else we will have liberty of opinion; and in all things we will operate in a climate of love.

Restoration of doctrine and unity were seen as means, not ends in themselves. The *end* to be achieved was evangelism that would sweep the world.

The Scriptures that rose to the surface and galvanized these ideas into a vigorous movement were those in which Jesus prayed for the unity and solidarity of His people in order that the world might be won:

My prayer is not for them [the first generation disciples] alone. I pray also for those who will believe in me through their message, that all of them may be one, Father, just as you are in me an I am in you. . . . May they be brought to complete unity to let the world know that you sent me and have loved them—even as you have loved me (John 17:20-23).

## Its Mission

About two-thirds of the world's people are pagans. They make no pretense of being Christian. About one-third of the world is nominally Christian, in all variety of churches. Five percent of the people are seriously committed to Christianity as they understand it. The restoration movement represents a fraction of less than one percent.

The restoration movement seeks to address and persuade three kinds of people:

1. *The committed*, in terms of restoring faith and practice to New Testament intentions and in terms of coming together on a common understanding of (and commitment to) the essentials of Christianity.
2. *The nominals*, in terms of serious commitment to Christ on His terms.
3. *The unreached*, in terms of discipleship to Christ as Lord.

In its early days, the movement communicated with all those people. They were convinced that the intention of God for His church *can* be ascertained from Scripture. The restorers under-

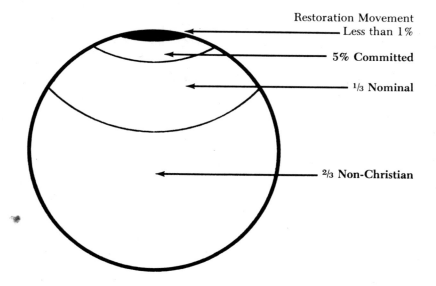

Figure 10-1. *Christianity and world population*

took a vigorous restudy of Scripture in order to understand it as it was first delivered and intended, not through the distortions of denominational creeds. As churches are restored in doctrine to common essentials and unified under those essentials, they thought, the world would be won to Christ to a much greater degree.

They became some of the most diligent and competent Biblical scholars of their day. They developed a hermeneutic that to this day is the most Biblically sound and consistent of any. They reconstructed the Biblical intent for the church, implementing it in such a way that the enterprise flourished. They also communicated their findings more persuasively than anyone in their generation. They studied and discussed concepts with people far and wide, on the public platform and personally—not always as adversaries, but as mutual seekers of Christ's will.

## The Result

"Churches sprang up everywhere like dandelions on a green lawn in spring."[1]

This is the way Donald McGavran describes the spread of the

restoration movement (of which he is a fifth-generation heir) during most of the nineteenth century. At its peak, the movement spread at such a pace that it has been cited as the fastest growing religious body on the North American continent.

The restorers found they could not wait for every item of restoration in doctrine to be worked through nor for unity to become a reality. When they turned their full attention to restoration and unity they developed conceptual clarity, but the movement stalled. But when they launched into vigorous evangelism as the leading edge for these other concerns, the movement generated enormous momentum. It exploded into growth *and* it made great strides in restoration of doctrine as well as unity. While evangelizing, they were searching the Scripture and seeking solidarity in the body of Christ. Under these circumstances, consensus developed on Scriptural intent and various groups swung together in unity.

Between 1830 and 1860 the movement's growth was "phenomenal," according to historian Howard Dentler.[2] Its membership grew by 900 percent while the population of the country grew only one-third as fast. Between 1860 and 1900, the movement grew another 500 percent—twice the rate of population growth. At the turn of the century, the movement was forty-five times as large as it had been seventy years earlier, vastly outstripping the growth of the population around it. America was being brought to the feet of Jesus Christ. The Great Commission was on the way to substantial fulfillment. At the turn of the century, churches were being planted at the rate of one thousand per year. That averages twenty new churches per week, or three per day! People were being baptized by the tens of thousands. Restoration was an idea whose time had come.

## Emerging Problems

In this movement, unity and restoration of doctrine were inextricably linked with evangelism as the frontline priority. The soundness of any doctrinal stance that did not lead to evangelism was spurious. Unity that did not lead to the same end was flawed.

Ironically—and tragically—the movement came upon hard times. It diverged into three streams. And it did so, I believe, largely because other issues shifted evangelism out of dominance. One stream, the Disciples of Christ, has declined more than twenty percent in each of the last two decades.[3] Another stream, the noninstrumental Churches of Christ, has moved out of a growth mode into a plateau and the beginning of decline, according to Flavil Yeakley.[4] The remaining stream appears to be holding its own; some statistics indicate encouraging growth is beginning. But it is far from establishing 1,000 churches per year, far from sweeping the world.

What happened to such a movement? It redefined faithfulness. One group redefined faithfulness as unity and refocused its priority there. Their efforts were absorbed in processes of merging with other groups into a stereotypical denomination, and into a maintenance mode. But focusing here throws the other concerns for evangelism and restoration of doctrine out of balance, and the dynamics no longer work. Concern for both restoration and evangelism fade.

Others in the movement redefined faithfulness as doctrinal purity. They have refined and refined their understandings of doctrine and have fractured into many additional subgroups in the process. As the lines of orthodoxy are drawn tighter, the core of the faithful, according to their definition, becomes smaller as more people are defined out. At its extreme, this process develops the idea that the narrower and more legalistic you get, the more carefully you define pure doctrine, the more faithful you are. Both unity and evangelism suffer.

## Real Faithfulness

Faithfulness has been defined in this book as maximum results in winning the world to Jesus and incorporating those who are won into the church as responsible members, where they grow and are transformed into God's creation intention. Neither unity nor sound doctrine ought to be compromised, but these concerns are best served in a context where the Great Commission mandate has priority. If either unity or doctrine is given priority the entire system breaks down. To the degree that the movement is not succeeding as it once did, it has shifted its focus from the original, authentic goals. Means and ends have become confused.

The restoration movement has, to some extent, succumbed to thinking "survival" rather than "success" on Christ's terms. It has tended to turn from pressing the victory of the kingdom to "building fences around the law." It has been inclined to take the Master's trust, bury it in the ground, and guard it. In a slow motion somersault, it has turned statically inward.

In so doing, the heirs of the movement have built walls of defense around themselves. Rather than addressing the peoples of the world, they have begun talking to each other about the people of the world outside. They say of the "committed" five percent, "Isn't it awful that they are in such confusion. What miserable enemies of the gospel—and of us!" They say of the "nominal" one-third, "Isn't it a shame that they wear the name of Christ but don't really mean it." Of the two-thirds who are totally without Christ, they say, "What a tragedy they are lost! What a shame that they think the way they do and live the way they do!"

Like the Pharisees, some Christians and churches congratulate themselves on their orthodoxy: "How can people really believe those other things? How dare they hold those doctrinal views!" Pharisaism justifies itself by criticizing the errors of others. It sets itself up to be a watchdog of orthodoxy rather than a producer of results in Christ's mandate. It redefines the church's role from one of movement to one of maintenance.

Christians need to be careful not to turn dynamic things into static things. During a recent series of chapel messages on the theme of holiness, everything that was said dealt with purity of life and attitude. But holiness includes more than just freedom from defilement.

The Jerusalem temple, for example, was to be holy. It was kept clean and undefiled not as an end in itself, but so the purposes of God could be accomplished there. It could be (and was, in many instances) kept ceremonially clean *without God's purpose being fulfilled in it.* Jewish custom went to extremes in striving for undefilement for which the productive purpose was lost. Until a holy thing is used its cleanliness is for nothing.

There is much spurious holiness in which people try to live lives free of the taint of the world, but they aren't accomplishing God's mission to any great degree. We can be pure and orthodox, but unproductive.

# Church Growth Eyes

Donald McGavran has coined the phrase, "Church Growth Eyes." He says we must look at the world constantly asking,

"Where are the lost? What can we do to reach them?"

"Where are the opportunities?"

"How can we produce maximum results for the kingdom?"

We must weigh every decision on the basis of whether or not it will help the church to succeed in its mission, thinking not of our preferences or prejudices, but of getting the job done. That is the way to look at the world through church growth eyes, seeing potential for growth and finding the way to get it done.

But if we are not careful we may be looking through maintenance eyes, saying, "We will bury our treasure and we will stand over it and guard it. We will keep a sharp lookout for every hint of heresy. We will scorn those who tolerate error. We will content ourselves with being small but pure. We may not accomplish much in bringing the peoples of the earth into the kingdom of our Lord, but we will stand firm. We will return the trust to the Master unsullied. And we will declare ourselves faithful."

The Lord says, "I will call you unfaithful, if that is what you do."

Morticians study "the restorative arts," cosmetic procedures that will restore the appearance of life to a dead body. But that is not sufficient for the restoration of the church of our Lord Jesus Christ. That body must not only be restored in form and appearance, but in vitality, in energy, in accomplishment. It is not enough for the church to be good, but good for nothing, like the third servant in the parable. There is no faithfulness without vigorous, intelligent effort to achieve God's goals. It would, I believe, be better to fail while giving God our best effort than to "succeed" by just playing it safe.

I am deeply concerned about churches who call themselves New Testament churches, but have only the form of godliness. They are static and unproductive, albeit orthodox in their own eyes. I am deeply concerned about rigidly static people who, with clenched jaw, affirm their faithfulness and pass judgment on all others who are "in error," by their definition.

Dr. McGavran says,

> Being a real New Testament church means believing and doing what the New Testament church did.... Today, in a world where three out of four persons have yet to believe in Jesus Christ and at least two out of every four have yet to hear of Jesus Christ, if a congregation is not reproducing, it is not a New Testament church, no matter what it calls itself![5]

In today's Church Growth movement, the concern for evangelism is so strong that restoration is occurring and people are converging in unity. People of many backgrounds have become so evangelistically convicted that they are searching the Scriptures for insights that will lead the church to be productive, restoring themselves to essential faith and practice, and converging in a consensus that further encourages evangelism.

## Summary

I believe that *no church is acceptably restored to the New Testament ideal if it is not committed to vigorous, intelligent, massive propagation of the kingdom in this world.*

The people who have had that dream for 180 years ought to be in the vanguard of this movement whose time has come—*again.*

[1] Donald McGavran, in a lecture to the Cincinnati Bible Seminary faculty and administration, May 12-13, 1981.

[2] Howard E. Dentler, "Statistical Profile of the Christian Church (Disciples of Christ)," in *The Christian Church (Disciples of Christ): An Interpretive Examination in the Cultural Context*, George G. Beasley, Jr., ed. (St. Louis: The Bethany Press, 1973), p. 308.

[3] Ibid., pp. 308, 309. See also James Mann, "New Life Ahead for Christian Unity," *U.S. News and World Report*, December 27, 1982/January 3, 1983, pp. 57, 58.

[4] Flavil R. Yeakley, Jr. *Why Churches Grow* (Christian Communications, Inc., 1979), p. 7.

[5] Donald McGavran and Winfield C. Arn, *Ten Steps for Church Growth* (San Francisco: Harper and Row, 1977), p. 96.

# A Time for Greatness

Several decades ago, historian Will Durant projected where the times were moving. He talked about civilization wandering off into the wastelands. He described a time like that which hungered for the birth of Christ. He was speaking of the times in which we now live.

Paul spoke of how Christ came when time reached a "fullness." The climate of the times was right for Him to come.

The restoration movement also began at such a moment in history. In a recent book, Max Ward Randall showed the many ways in which conditions were right for the restoration movement when it came on the scene of history.[1] The leaders of that movement set their sails to catch the winds that were blowing and used them to power the implementation of their grand vision of New Testament Christianity.

I believe that the last few years of the twentieth century may present an even more fruitful opportunity, perhaps the greatest in the history of the church. Conditions are right to press the success of the kingdom enterprise to its highest potential.

"It was the best of times, it was the worst of times." So Charles Dickens began *A Tale of Two Cities*. Ours, too, is an era of strangely mixed contradictions, of light and shadow; a kaleidoscope of change. But it is, for the kingdom, the best of times.

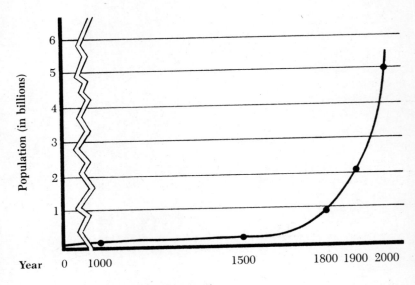

Figure 11-1. *World population growth*

# The World Scene

## The Population Explosion

At the time of Jesus, world population numbered some 200 million. From then, it took eighteen centuries for the population to each one billion. But the population then doubled in only *one century*. It doubled again in only *one-half century*. The present figure approaches five billion. It is projected that growth between now and the turn of the century will number a minimum of 93 million per year.

While world leaders are concerned with the enormous sociological problems that attend such growth, for Christians the challenge of reaching these people with the gospel of Christ is more imperative than any other concern. When one considers how small a minority of the peoples of the world have been reached with past and present evangelistic efforts, it is obvious that far greater determination, commitment, sacrifice, and sanctified intelligence will be required to keep pace.

One way of visualizing the size of the evangelistic task before us is through the "people group" concept. Ed Dayton points out that, of the more than three billion persons still unreconciled to God, only one billion live within cultures "where there are Christians who know Jesus and can share His love."[2] The remaining two billion can be further divided into about 16,750 different people groups—all totally unreached. Yet these represent but a part of the peoples still waiting to hear and respond to the gospel. The task is staggering. Nevertheless, reaching them is the core of the enterprise God has entrusted to us, His servants. And He is eager to empower us to do this task through His partnership and supernatural resources.

## Spiritual Conditions

In the past, American culture has tipped its hat to Biblical principles, even if it had no intention of living by them. The general attitude was, "If you want to be a Christian, that is fine. Everyone really ought to do that. It would be far better if we all lived by Biblical principles." But today our culture boldly rejects Biblical values and exalts alternatives, saying, "Who said those ways were right? I will live by the principles I have decided are right for me."

This state of affairs is creating a society that is more ready for evangelism than those earlier days of polite condescension toward Christianity. Our culture has come out of the fog of mushy thinking and has taken its stand by deliberate intent. Like the stiff-necked prodigal, our culture pursues the road it has chosen. But the pigsty lies inevitably in its path. The alternative it has chosen is being found bankrupt. Meaninglessness, hopelessness, and despair already drag at its heels. The flight to alcohol, other drugs, and sensual overload is a symptom of the intolerability of this condition.

Charles Mylander describes in vivid language the current world situation:

> Underlying the outward decline is a rejection of Christian values and the very idea of a moral law. When everything becomes relevant, including truth itself, society has no moorings, no roots, no footings.
> The moral breakdown touches every facet of human life. Broken homes shatter young lives with emotional trauma. Crime ravages not

only inner cities but suburbs and small towns. Dishonesty and greed undermine the economic system. Sexual immorality inflicts terrible psychological damage. Racism raises its ugly head of injustice. Respect for human life dwindles as the blood of aborted babies cries out from the ground. Most frightening of all is the attitude of the rank and file: "I don't care. Just leave me alone." Jesus predicted such a backlash of apathy when he said, "Because of the increase of wickedness, the love of most will grow cold" (Matthew 24:12, NIV).

Moral decline, however, is accompanied by a renewed interest in the supernatural. . . . The desire for supernatural help with life's struggles reflects the common despair with human solutions. Optimistic promises of spiritual progress by human achievement taste sweet but turn bitter in the stomach.[3]

Satan's counterfeit never works. It is eventually revealed as the fraud that it is. The recurring swings from rebellion to revival gain momentum from the fact that our attempts to live by other than God's ways are, without exception, found unworkable and intolerable. The optimism of humanism is being demonstrated to be unfounded. One fact is becoming inescapably clear: we cannot order life and society on the secular model we have been trying to use.

The pendulum swing of rebellion and return to God may have already reached its farthest point and be on the way back. It is possible that we are entering what could be *the* revival of twenty centuries, a revival that is long overdue.

From a worldwide perspective, observers are describing people as remarkably receptive to the gospel. The present conditions of rebellion and despair tend to plow up people's souls and make them ready for the seed of the gospel. The fluid, uprooted, open-to-change qualities of today's society make the whole population ready for "people movements."

Recent Gallup polls characterize America as in a "deep religious renewal." Never have there been so many unreached but winnable people in the world. George Gallup sees today

a spiritual quest of fast-growing proportions. . . . People in all walks of life are hungry for depth and meaning in their lives and want to gain a new understanding of their relationship to God. . . .

We certainly have the elements that could made for an explosion in faith in this country.[4]

Another Gallup study showed an increasing trust in religion even in the midst of explosive scientific and technological advancement. At the root of this change, said Gallup, is the "growing conviction that religion, rather than science, can answer the problems of the world."[5]

U.S. News and World Report made similar diagnoses and projections for the next half century.[6]

Americans are seeking answers different from the false promises of secular humanism and advancing technology. They may be more responsive to an uncluttered, undistorted Biblical Christianity than to any other option. This same hunger for meaning, however, makes them easy prey for false prophets unless reached with the true gospel.

America's self-admitted pagans are ready for God's alternative, to a degree that makes this a "five-talent time" in which we labor.

## The Church Scene

Some people assume that America is largely churched, but that is not true. Statistics vary, but it appears that 80 million Americans make no pretense of faith. They are admittedly secular pagans. Another 70 million are no more than nominal members of denominations of all varieties.[7] That means there are at least 150 million Americans effectively unreached, and that says nothing of the millions who are churched but in such error that correction is needed. Fully three-quarters of the people in most American communities are yet to be reached for the kingdom. Worldwide, only about five percent of the people are serious practicing Christians, if one takes Christian in its broadest sense.

The mainline denominational churches have (with some notable exceptions) been in a state of plateau or skidding decline. This trend has not been reserved for liberal denominations alone. Even many biblically-oriented churches are in holding patterns.

Religion as a merely human enterprise is failing, clearing the way for revitalization—perhaps a new awakening that will prove to be the greatest in history. Liberalism, ecumenism, the social gospel, and habitual denominational loyalties are waning.

On the other hand, many individual church members are seek-

105

ing a return to the dynamic Christianity of the New Testament. They are not necessarily dissatisfied with the church, but with the mediocrity of the congregations of which they are a part. Much of this stirring to vitality centers among the youth and young families. While it is not difficult to motivate them toward significant goals, it is increasingly difficult to rally their support for activities they perceive as pointless. Passive churches, says church growth expert Lyle Schaller, are "doomed to be seen as irrelevant by at least half of all the persons born between 1945 and 1970."[8]

Turning from his observations on the world situation, Charles Mylander is equally forthright in his evaluation of Christian trends:

> More and more often God's people are forced to take an unmistakable stand for Christian morality and against dishonesty and indecency. The hazy grays of nominal Christianity are disappearing like the morning fog, and light and darkness contrast more starkly all the time.[9]

The churches that are in trouble today are those marked by routine, business as usual, preservation of human traditions, or maintenance of themselves as institutions. Churches with a keen sense of mission as God's agency in the world, acting in concert with God for achieving His mighty purpose, are finding new life and vitality. People from many backgrounds find themselves converging as they approach Scripture rather than defending historical differences of viewpoint.

Another situation churches must face is the shifting population in America. Some geographical areas are declining in population while others are growing rapidly. New churches by the thousands must be established in the growing areas to reach these relocating people.

## The Resource Explosion

Never have our available resources been so abundant. Research has brought our knowledge and our tools for effectiveness in Christ's work to their highest level of development in history. The Church Growth movement is largely responsible for this explosion, with its emphasis on research and publication. Off the printing presses of America rolls a constant stream of literature offering insight and practical help for the work of the church.

Training opportunities for ministers and other church leaders are becoming ever more plentiful and available. Workshops and seminars of high quality are multiplying, along with seminary programs tailored to the special needs and schedules of full-time ministers. Higher competence in ministry is within the grasp of more ministers than ever before.

Christians and churches have more wealth at their disposal than at any time in twenty centuries. The worldwide enterprise for Christ can be powerfully underwritten whenever Christians decide it has a high enough priority.

Developments in communication and transportation have put practically every person on the globe within reaching distance for the gospel. With the exception of the totalitarian countries, all the world is accessible. Even some of the closed countries are becoming more open.

There has never been greater potential for effective strategies in fulfilling Christ's program for the world.


## A Five-Talent Time

In worship not long ago, I was struck by Anne Ortlund's words as the congregation sang her hymn, "Macedonia." This song should become the theme for today's churches: "The vision of a dying world is vast before our eyes. . . . O Lord, constrain and move Thy church the glad news to impart! And Lord, as Thou dost stir Thy church, begin within my heart."

Ours is a time for greatness, a wonderful five-talent opportunity for magnificent progress in the Master's enterprise!

The church needs men who, knowing the world around them, and knowing the Christ above them and within, will set the trumpet of the Gospel to their lips, and proclaim His sovereignty and all sufficiency. . . . "The whole creation," wrote Paul, "waits with eager longing for the sons of God to be revealed." It is listening for the sound of a distant pilgrim chorus, the march of a great consecrated brotherhood in Christ, the decisive emergence of a new race, the true sons of God sealed with the cross. It is scanning the roads down which that ransomed host, that nobler breed of saints, shall come at destiny's hour to bring history to its fulfillment. . . . Go forth, then, in the heartening assurance that this present cataclysmic hour is alive with spiritual potentialities.[10]

## Summary

Never has the need been so great, never the opportunity so great, and never our capability so great for achieving God's purpose. It is a five-talent time.

---

[1] Max Ward Randall, *The Great Awakenings and the Restoration Movement* (Joplin, MO: College Press, 1983).

[2] Ed Dayton, *That Everyone May Hear* (Monrovia, CA: MARC, 1983), p. 13.

[3] Charles Mylander, *Secrets for Growing Churches* (San Francisco: Harper and Row), pp.. 48, 49.

[4] "Measuring the State of Religion," *The Lookout*, August 8, 1982, p. 12.

[5] Bruce Buursma, "Poll Shows Americans Placing Trust in God," *The Cincinnati Enquirer*, January 1, 1984.

[6] "What Will the Next 50 Years Bring: A Search for Life's Meaning in High-Tech Era," *U.S. News and World Report*, May 9, 1983.

[7] Donald McGavran and George Hunter, *Church Growth Strategies That Work* (Nashville: Abingdon, 1980), p. 20.

[8] Lyle E. Schaller, *Activating the Passive Church* (Nashville: Abingdon Press, 1981), p. 14.

[9] Mylander, op. cit., p. 50.

[10] James S. Stewart, *Heralds of God* (London: Hodder and Stoughton, 1946), pp. 12, 13, 25, 26.

CHAPTER 12

# Getting Under Way

"What do I do now?"

"Where can I take hold and begin?"

This chapter will suggest some principles and resources for accelerating the progress of God's enterprise at your church.

Ways and means for accomplishing the Master's enterprise must be homemade, hammered out by the people involved in a specific time and place. Most of the suggestions in this chapter are addressed to churches and their leaders. Individual Christians, however, will also find possibilities for personal growth.

## A Place to Begin

Permeate the thinking of your congregation with the concepts of this book in the following ways:

The following leadership groups should prayerfully work through this book and its companion volume, *The Church On Purpose*, with a special consciousness for how the concepts apply to your congregation: (1) The minister and staff members; (2) elders and deacons; (3) teachers, officers, and other leaders.

Where possible, meet in groups of eight to fifteen persons. One person should coordinate this procedure so that there is consistency and communication between groups.

This phase can be carried out in weekly sessions or in retreats. Participants should thoroughly digest the concepts for themselves and the congregation. Each person should have and read his own book, but he must process the ideas with others if significant results are going to occur. A total of twelve to fifteen hours of interaction time will be necessary for a group to process the ideas.

Second, arrange for the entire congregation to study this book in groups of eight to fifteen and discuss its ideas. This might be done over a series of weeks in Sunday-school classes, midweek Bible studies, or specially formulated groups, or in a concentrated method at an all-church retreat. Such a study must be well organized and seriously carried out in order to involve a maximum number of the congregation. It is imperative that a "common mind" develop throughout the congregation regarding these matters. The leaders who have already been through the process can now become leaders of these study/discussion groups.

This phase can be carried out in a total of six to ten hours of interaction time with each group. The sessions should be spaced far enough apart to give participants time to read and digest the concepts. Absorption that leads to action cannot be hurried.

Next, appoint an ongoing task force to give direction in developing specific strategies to fulfill Jesus' mandate. This body should become the keystone that provides direction to the whole life and work of the congregation and provides cohesion among all other committees or boards. Ideally, therefore, it should consist of the minister and other salaried staff members, the elders, and other key people. Accelerating the progress of the enterprise must always be their top priority. They must guard this priority and never allow other matters to crowd it out.

This early phase is of critical importance. It is foundational to everything that follows. But it is only the beginning. Next it will be necessary to develop specific ways and means for individual Christians and the congregation to carry out the following goals of the enterprise:

*Goal One:* Winning as many people as possible to become disciples of Jesus Christ and responsible members of your congregation.

*Goal Two:* Helping to win as many as possible in other localities, through the multiplying of mission work and new American congregations.

*Goal Three:* Helping every Christian incorporate into his life details of God's intentions so that he is transformed into Christlikeness, and a progressively deeper personal relationship with God.

*Goal Four:* Equipping every Christian to find and fulfill his role in the congregation as a responsible member of the body of Christ.

*Goal Five:* Equipping every Christian to function as God's agent in all his contacts with the world around him and in every context—family, social, community, and work.

Goals One and Two are directly evangelistic. Goals Three, Four, and Five are nurture goals but they, too, must deliberately include evangelism as an outcome.

The most comprehensive resources for effective ways and means come from The Institute for American Church Growth.[2] A number of their resources, along with others, will be described below. Some of them may represent theological backgrounds different from your own. However, they can still offer insights, principles, and examples that can be adapted to your congregation. Mature church leaders can glean from many sources, incorporating ideas that are compatible with their situations and convictions, and rejecting those that are not.

## Ways and Means: Goal One

Local evangelism occurs through three channels: (1) Spontaneous witnessing of Christians to their family members, friends, neighbors, and other associates; (2) an ongoing program of systematic identifying, cultivating, teaching, persuading, and winning unreached persons; and (3) attracting and reaching people through the various activities of the church, such as the worship service, classes and groups, or special ministries.

### Spontaneous Witnessing

The finest resource for developing spontaneous evangelism by the general membership is a program developed by The Institute for American Church Growth.[2] Called *The Master's Plan for*

*Making Disciples*, it helps the local church build a unique community of believers into a cohesive disciple-making power base—working together, praying together, and encouraging one another in the process of reaching out to those special people God has already brought into their lives. It does not involve a memorized witnessing scheme, but emphasizes an attitude and lifestyle in which Christians live out and communicate their faith simply and naturally.

The Master's Plan centers in a comprehensive action kit of administrative and teaching materials. An accompanying videotape is encouraging and motivational. The Institute also conducts seminars for church leaders at several locations around the country as a way of introducing *The Master's Plan*. Consultants are available to come into local churches to initiate the program.

## Systematic Program of Evangelism

It appears that in most congregations about ten percent of the members are gifted evangelists. That is, these people are motivated and capable (with organization and training) of calling, communicating the gospel systematically, and persuading others to become Christians. These people should be identified, trained, and mobilized into a regular program of calling.

Many churches have adapted the Evangelism Explosion[3] program to this purpose. The manual is especially useful in organizing an evangelistic program and training callers in effective interaction.

The Institute for American Church Growth has developed a program and materials for identifying people who are most receptive to becoming Christians, responding to their needs, incorporating them into your congregation, and monitoring their growth and development. It is called *The Caring System*.

For the content of the gospel message, two resources are particularly useful. One is John Hendee's *Ambassadors for Christ* materials.[4] The program includes a trainer's manual and a student manual. The trainer's manual is a guide for the leader in conducting a training program and deploying the trainees in evangelistic calling. The student's manual is a workbook for the training sessions and a reference manual for callers. The heart of the program is a pamphlet called *A Peace Treaty With God*.

Another valuable resource for training callers is a videotape by Tim Coop called *How to Share Your Faith.* [5] It provides training in communicating a highly comprehensive and persuasive explanation of what it means to become a Christian.

## Attracting People to Your Church

The field of church growth is essentially a study of how churches provide for evangelistic growth and become magnetic to new people. Two books lay the foundations in this area—Peter Wagner's *Your Church Can Grow*[6] and *Ten Steps for Church Growth* by Donald McGavran and Win Arn.[7] These principles are also articulated in a clear and practical way by Ben Merold, minister of one of the country's most effective churches in a videotape, *Principles of Church Growth.*[8] Reeves and Jenson link strategies with the principles in their book, *Always Advancing: Modern Strategies for Church Growth.*[9] This book is in the "must read" category for persons who lead and plan for a congregation.

A rapid way to discover new growth potential for your congregation is *The Church Growth Opportunity Check-Up* from The Institute for American Church Growth.

A more elaborate approach is provided by the Church Growth Diagnostic Clinic developed by the Charles E. Fuller Institute of Evangelism and Church Growth.[10] Information on this and other resources provided by the Institute are available upon request.

To help the entire congregation catch the vision of the Church Growth point of view, The Institute for American Church Growth has a twelve-week adult Sunday-school curriculum, *Let the Church Grow!* For leadership level people, the Institute offers workshops and seminars at locations across the country.

The Institute also has materials for a high-visibility outreach event called *A Celebration of Friendship.* The program provides an opportunity for members to introduce their unchurched friends and relatives to your congregation in a setting that is not "hard sell" evangelism.

Many churches are rediscovering the Sunday school as a readily available channel for implementing many aspects of evangelism and nurture. The Institute for American Church Growth has developed a program to help capitalize on this valuable tool—*A New Vision: Sunday School Growth Kit.*

# Ways and Means: Goal Two

Mission works in other parts of the world and new churches in other parts of America do not spring up on their own. People like you and churches like yours cause this kind of expansion of the kingdom to occur.

## Church Planting in America

Population growth, neglected areas, neglected peoples, and population shifts make vigorous church planting *imperative*. In many areas of the country church planting organizations already exist. You can deploy funds and people to help them intensify their good work. Or you may find that new churches are necessary in your own community to reach those your congregation cannot reach. In this case your congregation becomes responsible to "mother" a new church, either on your own or in collaboration with other area churches.

Evangelizing America may require existing churches not only to invest money, but to challenge their people to invest their lives in these efforts. Many Christians, for example, are in a position to take early retirement—think of the resource they represent if they were to direct their lives to establishing new churches or taking up mission work! A number of Bible colleges and seminaries will help such persons rapidly train to make their remaining years significant in this way.

In addition to the resources for church planting listed in the bibliography, The Institute for American Church Growth has collected practical materials into a program called *The Great Commission Church Planting Kit*.

## Missions to Other Countries

Much of what has been said about establishing new congregations in America can also be said here. A large number of missionary enterprises could multiply their effectiveness if American Christians would become sacrificial and "lavish" in their support.

Many more missionaries must be recruited and trained. These persons must come from congregations like yours. The colleges and seminaries to train them must be supported by individuals and congregations like yours.

Inform your people about the mission works that you support. Keep information flowing constantly through all channels in your congregation. Increasingly, members of supporting congregations have the opportunity to visit their missions and work there for a short term.

Faith-Promise programs are effective for developing missions financial support in congregations. Robert Reeves has written the definitive manual on the Faith-Promise approach.[11]

## Ways and Means: Goal Three

In addition to Bible study and prayer, Christians need three levels of interaction with each other if maximum transformation of their lives is to occur.

### Corporate Worship

Worship services consist of celebrative praise to God and effective meeting of people's needs. They must be carefully planned around deliberate strategies to fulfill these purposes. All aspects of the worship service—greetings at the door, ushering, Communion, singing, preaching, reading Scripture, offerings, prayer, and even the announcements—must not only deal with the minds of the worshipers, but also touch people's hearts, fire their imaginations, and move their wills.

Worship is usually conducted with Christians in mind, but the "outsider" must also be considered. Most interested non-Christians form their impressions of Christianity by what the church does in the Sunday morning worship time. Therefore, the worship service must also be planned and conducted with them in mind, too.

Resources for worship are listed in the bibliography. The audio tapes by Rick Warren are especially stimulating.

### Participation

Christians who are involved only in the corporate worship of the congregation usually remain peripheral and subject to becoming dropouts. They need to be significantly involved in some ongoing sub-entity such as a Sunday-school class, women's or men's organization, choir, committee, or task force.

Christians must be involved in such a way that they are known by name, recognized when they are present, missed when they are absent, and provided a means for Christian activity.

This is one of the most important functions of Sunday-school classes—probably equally important as the teaching. As a resource for the Sunday school, keep in mind the program kit from The Institute for American Church Growth: *A New Vision: Sunday School Growth*. The Institute also has *The Dynamic Sunday School* film series.

An additional program from the Institute provides ways to assimilate members into the body of Christ. *The Shepherd's Guide to Caring and Keeping* is a six-week study based on the film *See You Sunday?* and leads a special task force through key areas of priority in developing an effective strategy for membership incorporation into the church body.

## Fellowship

Fellowship is more than socializing. Fellowship occurs when people know each other so intimately that they can share joys, sorrows, victories, and problems, and provide spiritual, emotional, and social support to one another. Persons in this kind of fellowship become "accountability partners," helping each other remain faithful and continue growing. Seldom can this depth of relationship exist with more than six to ten other people.

People sometimes argue for smallness of churches on the basis of the need for fellowship. However, most people can maintain a casual acquaintance with only about sixty people and a really personal relationship with six to ten. A Christian does not need to know everybody in the church even on a casual level, but it is imperative that every person know *some* other Christians in the congregation on a deeply personal level. If this is the case, then a congregation of ten thousand is not too large.

The Institute for American Church Growth has developed a series of resources under the title *Who Cares About Love?* It is based on the realization that *the* most important command of Christ to His disciples is to love. When the priority of love is lacking in a congregation, the goal of making disciples will never be effectively reached. Visitors will not return when they do not encounter a genuine sense of caring and love among the members.

The resource consists of two films, a book, and a "Church Action Kit." The components can be used separately or together as a means of establishing the foundational requirement for a growing church—genuine love for each other and for others outside the church.

Sometimes Sunday-school classes can provide the necessary fellowship, but not always. Larger Sunday-school classes sometimes have sub-groups for fellowship.

Often home groups provide the best opportunity for high-quality Christian fellowship to develop. These groups also have the potential for evangelism if this dimension is desired and provided for. Multiplying of such groups is rapidly becoming obvious as a key strategy for qualitative and quantitative church growth.

Research consistently demonstrates that churches grow in size and quality as they constantly multiply groups. Groups can focus on Bible study, prayer, Christian fellowship, or on some kind of ministry or task. Some groups specialize in one of these areas; others combine more than one.

Roberta Hestenes has written the definitive manual on small group programs in the local church: *Building Christian Community Through Small Groups.*[12] Other resources for working with fellowship groups are included in the bibliography.

## Ways and Means: Goal Four

Many growing, vigorous churches are helping their members recapture the Biblical emphasis on Christians finding fulfillment and effectiveness in the service for which God has prepared them and the church has trained them.

Again, The Institute for American Church Growth has developed systematic ways of dealing with this concept. One program is called *Spiritual Gifts for Building the Body*. Leaders who are considering this program (as with any program) will want to evaluate it and adapt it as necessary to be congruent with their theological convictions. Another program is called the *Mobilizing Laity for Ministry Church Action Kit*. Yet another goes by the name *Disciples in the Making*. The Institute also has a collection of films under the title, *Dynamic Laity Film Series*.

# Ways and Means: Goal Five

All the previous suggestions in this chapter should help to achieve this goal. However, Christians have many other ministries to fulfill in their contacts with the world.

One special resource will be of particular help. Robert E. Korth, in a book to be released later this year by Standard Publishing, has collected examples of Christians undertaking specialized ministries to the people around them. It will spark plenty of ideas about what kinds of ministry opportunities are open to you.

---

[1]Cincinnati: Standard Publishing, 1982.

[2]The Institute for American Church Growth, 709 East Colorado Blvd., Suite 150, Pasadena, CA 91101. Founded and headed by Dr. Win Arn. A non-denominational organization specializing in applying church growth study and research to practice in the field. It provides area seminars, local church consultations and seminars, and a broad variety of program materials for use in local churches.

The Institute produces two journals: *Church Growth Resource News* (a tabloid describing their services and materials and listing scheduled seminars) and *The Win Arn Growth Report* (keeping readers abreast of concepts in church growth). Both are free. You may write them for information or telephone 1-800-423-4844 (in California, call 818-449-4400.)

[3]D. James Kennedy, *Evangelism Explosion* (Wheaton, Illinois: Tyndale House Publishers, 1970).

[4]Cincinnati: Standard Publishing, 1984.

[5]The videotape, consisting of three thirty-minute sessions, is available from Good News Productions International, 2111 N. Main St., P.O. Box 222, Joplin, MO 64802 (telephone 417-782-0060). You may write for a complete catalog of their materials.

[6]Glendale, California: Regal Books, 1976.

[7]San Francisco: Harper and Row, Publishers, 1977.

[8]The videotape consists of four thirty-minute sessions, and can be rented or purchased from Good News Productions International at the above address.

[9]San Bernadino, California: Here's Life Publishers, 1984.

[10]You may write for a list of resources and services to P.O. Box 989, Pasadena, CA 91102.

[11]*Faith Promise: A Mission Success Story* (Cincinnati: Standard Publishing).

[12]Available through the bookstore, Fuller Theological Seminary, 135 N. Oakland Ave., Pasadena, CA 91101. Published in 1984.

[13]Cincinnati: Standard Publishing, 1986.

# Bibliography

The books, programs, and tapes listed in the previous chapter are prime resources. They are not listed again in the following supplementary bibliography.

The assumption that one can learn from sources with which he does not totally agree should be particularly applied to the resources below. They are listed because they have value for further study in the effort to be more productive in the Master's enterprise.

This bibliography is by no means exhaustive. It is but a sampling of the vast resources available today.

One of the most stimulating resources consists of a set of tapes by Rick Warren, minister of the Saddleback Valley Community Church. His first set deals with preaching, worship, evangelism, and leadership. Several other sets have become available since then.

You may direct requests for lists and prices to Church Growth Secretary, Saddleback Valley Community Church, 25401 Cabot, Suite 215, Laguna Hills, CA 92653; telephone (714) 581-5683.

# Foundational Works and General Resources

Dudley, Roger L., and Des Cummings, Jr. *Adventures in Church Growth.* Washington, DC: Review and Herald Publishing Co., 1983. Insights into church growth learned by Seventh-Day Adventists. Many concepts are transferable to other churches.

Gibbs, Eddie. *I Believe in Church Growth.* Grand Rapids, MI: William B. Eerdmans Publishing Co., 1982. A substantial general text in the field of church growth.

Hunter, Kent R. *Foundations for Church Growth.* New Haven, MO: Leader Publishing Co., 1983. Application of church growth principles to Lutheran churches. Many concepts transferable to other churches.

Hunter, Kent R., ed. *Your Church Has Personality.* Nashville: Abingdon Press, 1985. A philosophy of ministry based on the concept that every congregation has a unique personality that must be considered in planning for the future. Tells how to establish a philosophy of ministry.

Jenson, Ron, and Jim Stevens. *Dynamics of Church Growth.* Grand Rapids, MI: Baker Book House, 1981. A summary of church growth principles and application to the local church.

McGavran, Donald. *Understanding Church Growth.* Grand Rapids, MI: William B. Eerdmans Publishing Co., 1980. The definitive work on church growth, the best of the thinking of the founder of the church growth point of view. It is important to secure the 1980 edition rather than an earlier one.

McGavran, Donald, and Win Arn. *Back to Basics in Church Growth.* Wheaton, IL: Tyndale House, 1981. A Biblical perspective on church growth, so related to the spiritual dimension that it could be read as a devotional exercise. Excellent for introducing the basic imperative for growth to non-growing congregations.

Schaller, Lyle E. *Activating the Passive Church.* Nashville: Abingdon Press, 1981. The nature, cause, and cure for passivity in churches. A "must read" book for church leaders.

Wagner, C. Peter. *Leading Your Church to Growth.* Ventura, CA: Regal Books, 1984. An important study for understanding leader-follower relationships in order to develop dynamic churches.

Wagner, C. Peter. *Your Church Can Be Healthy.* Nashville: Abingdon Press, 1979. A description and prescription for eight common "diseases" that hamper the growth of congregations. This book, along with another by Wagner, *Your Church Can Grow* (see notes in Chapter 12), belong on the "must read" list for church leaders.

Watson, David. *I Believe in Evangelism*. Grand Rapids, MI: William B. Eerdmans Publishing Co., 1976. Application of the Great Commission to today's opportunities.

## Spontaneous Personal Evangelism

Aldrich, Joseph. *Life-Style Evangelism*. Portland, OR: Multnomah Press, 1981.

Green, Michael. *Evangelism in the Early Church*. Grand Rapids, MI: William B. Eerdmans Publishing Co., 1970. An exhaustive study of how evangelism exploded across the Roman world in the first two centuries. The best researched and most complete book on the subject.

McGavran, Donald. *The Bridges of God*. New York: Friendship Press, 1981. McGavran's early thinking on how individuals act as bridges over which the gospel flows to the people in their web of contacts.

Yeakley, Flavil R. *Why Churches Grow*. Christian Communications, (2001-B W. Detroit, Broken Arrow, OK 74012), 1979. This research identified personal influence between friends as the key to effective evangelism. It also tells how to establish conditions in the church to enhance evangelism and to identify persons most likely to be responsive to evangelism. A "must read" book for church leaders.

## Programs and Conditions for Effective Church Growth

Arn, Win, ed. *The Pastor's Church Growth Handbook*, Volumes I and II. Pasadena, CA: Church Growth Press, 1979. A compendium of short articles from many sources, with many "how-to" suggestions.

Dunkin, Steve. *Church Advertising*. Nashville: Abingdon Press, 1982.

Engel, James. *Contemporary Christian Communication: Its Theory and Practice*. Nashville: Thomas Nelson Publishers, 1979. Application of communication theory to communicating the gospel to the world.

Engel, James F., and Wilbert H. Norton. *What's Gone Wrong With the Harvest?* Grand Rapids, MI: Zondervan Publishing Co., 1975. Investigation of the failure of the church to communicate persuasively to the world around it; suggests how communications can be improved.

Hale, J. Russell. *The Unchurched: Who They Are and Why They Stay Away*. San Francisco: Harper and Row, 1980.

Hunter, George G., III. *The Contagious Congregation*. Nashville Abingdon Press, 1979.

Johnson, Ben. *An Evangelism Primer: Practical Principles for Congregations*. Atlanta: John Knox Press, 1983. Simple guidelines and useful tools for developing a program of evangelism in a local church.

Johnson, Douglas W. *Reaching Out to the Unchurched.* Valley Forge, PA: Judson Press, 1983.

Kotler, Philip. *Marketing for Nonprofit Organizations.* Englewood Cliffs, NJ: Prentice-Hall, Inc. 1982. Application of marketing concepts to non-commercial institutions: finding and meeting needs, researching your field, planning, analyzing the people you are trying to reach, "marketing" ideas. Extremely relevant to churches.

McGavran, Donald, and George Hunter III. *Church Growth Strategies That Work.* Nashville: Abingdon Press, 1980. An excellent introduction to the church growth movement. It also provides practical ways to motivate people for growth, train the membership, and help small churches grow.

Murray, Dick. *Strengthening the Adult Sunday School Class.* Nashville: Abingdon Press, 1981. Since the adult Sunday-school class represents great potential as a means of organizing, equipping, and mobilizing Christians, this book is of great importance.

Mylander, Charles. *Secrets for Growing Churches.* San Francisco: Harper and Row, 1979.

Schaller, Lyle E. *Effective Church Planning.* Nashville: Abingdon Press, 1983. Practical assistance in how to make plans for the church. One among a large number of excellent books from this prolific author and practical church consultant. Church leaders should become acquainted with his other books as well.

Schaller, Lyle E. *Assimilating New Members.* Nashville: Abingdon Press, 1978. How the congregation can develop evangelistic drawing power to attract and win new people.

Tucker, Grayson L. *A Church Planning Questionnaire: Manual and Discoveries from 100 Churches.* Available from the bookstore of Louisville Presbyterian Seminary, 1044 Alta Vista, Louisville, KY 40205. Enables church leaders to discover important characteristics of their congregations as a basis for planning in order to meet real needs and help the church to develop. Sets forth important concepts as well as the tools for assessing them.

Waymire, Bob, and C. Peter Wagner. *The Church Growth Survey Handbook.* Global Church Growth (P.O. Box 66, Santa Clara, CA 95052), 1983. A tool for studying the growth history and making growth projections for a local church.

Werning, Waldo J. *Vision and Strategy for Church Growth.* Grand Rapids, MI: Baker Book House, 1983. The role of leadership in church growth. The place of spiritual discipline, spirituality, goal setting, use of members in ministry. An extensive appendix provides ideas, questionnaires, and charts as tools to carefully evaluate the past and prepare for the future.

# Growth for the Smaller Church

Crandall, Ronald K., and L.Ray Sells. *There's New Life in the Small Congregation*. Nashville: Discipleship Resources, 1983. Order direct by writing to Box 840, Nashville, TN 37202.

Dudley, Carl S. *Making the Small Church Effective*. Nashville: Abingdon Press, 1978. Not necessarily a growth oriented book, but it explains many of the dynamics of small churches.

Grubbs, Bruce, ed. *Helping a Small Church Grow*. Nashville: Convention Press, 1980.

Maner, Robert E. *Making the Small Church Grow*. Kansas City, MO: Beacon Hill Press, 1982. How one Nazarene church broke the barriers of smallness in order to grow.

Zunkel, C. Wayne. *Growing the Small Church: A Guide for Church Leaders*. Elgin, IL: David C. Cook, 1982.


# Planting New Churches

Amberson, Talmadge R., ed. *The Birth of Churches: The Biblical Basis for Church Planting*. Nashville: Broadman Press, 1979. Not a "how to" book, but this provides the Biblical and theological basis for planting new churches.

Chaney, Charles L. *Church Planting in America at the End of the Twentieth Century*. Wheaton, IL: Tyndale House, 1982. One of the best contemporary books on the subject.

Falwell, Jerry, and Elmer Towns. *Stepping Out On Faith*. Wheaton, IL: Tyndale House, 1984. Case studies of 11 Baptist churches and discussion of spiritual gifts in that context.

Jones, Ezra Earl. *Strategies for New Churches*. San Francisco: Harper and Row, 1976. A practical guide for new church planting, based on experience.

Moorhous, Carl W. *Growing New Churches: Step-by-Step Procedures in New Church Planting*. Cincinnati: Standard Publishing, 1975. Practical guidelines from one of today's most experienced church planters.

Redford, F.J. *Planting New Churches*. Nashville: Broadman Press, 1979.

Rust, Brian, and Barry McLeish. *The Support-Raising Handbook: A Guide for Christian Workers*. Downers Grove, IL: InterVarsity Press, 1984.

Towns, Elmer L. *Getting a Church Started*. 1982. Available from the author at Liberty Baptist Seminary, Lynchburg, VA. This is a student manual used by Towns at Liberty Baptist Seminary, where church planting is at the heart of the curriculum. Very practical.

# Planting Churches Cross-Culturally

Brock, Charles. *The Principles and Practice of Indigenous Church Planting*. Nashville: Broadman Press, 1981.

Greenway, Roger, ed. *Guidelines for Urban Church Planting*. Grand Rapids, MI: Baker Book House, 1976.

Hesselgrave, David J. *Planting Churches Cross-Culturally*. Grand Rapids, MI: Baker Book House, 1980.

# Equipping Christians for Growth and Service

Harper, Michael. *Let My People Grow*. Plainfield, NJ: Logos International, 1977. Concept of leadership in an every-member ministry context.

Staton, Knofel. *Discovering My Gifts for Service*. Cincinnati: Standard Publishing, 1978.

Ver Straten, Charles A. *How to Start Lay Shepherding Ministries*. Grand Rapids, MI: Baker Book House, 1983.

Watson, David. *Called and Committed: World-Changing Discipleship*. Wheaton, IL: Harold Shaw Publishers, 1982. A call to decisive discipleship on the part of the "average" Christian.

Wilson, Marlene. *How to Mobilize Church Volunteers*. Minneapolis: Augsburg Publishing House, 1983. How to link people with tasks. Extensive questionnaires and other tools.

# Christian Fellowship and Small Groups

Barker, Steve, et. al. *Good Things Come in Small Groups*. Downers Grove, IL: InterVarsity Press, 1985. A book on small groups, written by a small group.

Cho, Paul Yonggi, and Harold Hostetler. *Successful Home Cell Groups*. Plainfield, NJ: Logos International, 1981. Describes how the world's largest church functions through cell groups. While written in the context of the Full Gospel Central Church in Seoul, Korea, it is relevant to other circumstances.

Crabb, Lawrence J., Jr., and Dan B. Allender. *Encouragement: The Key to Caring*. Grand Rapids, MI: Zondervan Publishing House, 1984. Written by one of today's most able Christian counselors, this is a useful book for improving Christian relationships.

Griffin, Em. *Getting Together: A Guide for Good Groups*. Downers Grove, IL: InterVarsity Press, 1982.

Hestenes, Roberta. *Using the Bible in Groups*. Philadelphia: Westminster Press, 1985.

Johnson, David W., and Frank P. Johnson. *Joining Together*. Englewood Cliffs, NJ: Prentice-Hall, 1982.

Kunz, Marilyn, and Catherine Schell. *How to Start a Neighborhood Bible study*. Dobbs Ferry, NY: Neighborhood Bible Studies, 1966. Address: Box 222, Dobbs Ferry, NY 10522. This book is also available with a cassette tape from Tyndale House Publishers, Wheaton, IL.

Nyquist, James F. *Leading Bible Discussions*. Downers Grove, IL: Inter-Varsity Press, 1967.

O'Connor, Elizabeth. *Journey Inward, Journey Outward*. New York: Harper and Row, 1968.

Peace, Richard. *Small Group Evangelism*. Downers Grove, IL: Inter-Varsity Press, 1985.

Smith, T.A. *Discovering Discipleship*. Cincinnati: Standard Publishing, 1980. A workbook for new Christians to study in small groups.

# Preaching

Chartier, Myron R. *Preaching as Communication*. Nashville: Abingdon Press, 1981.

Craddock, Fred. *As One Without Authority*. Nashville: Abingdon Press, 1979.

Craddock, Fred. *Preaching*. Nashville: Abingdon Press, 1985.

Griffin, Em. *The Mind Changers*. Wheaton, IL: Tyndale House, 1976.

Harding, Joe A. *Have I Told You Lately: Preaching to Help People and Churches Grow*. Church Growth Press (150 South Los Robles, #600, Pasadena, CA 91101), 1982.

Lewis, Ralph E. *Persuasive Preaching Today*. Wilmore, KY: Asbury Theological Seminary, 1979.

Lewis, Ralph E., and Gregg Lewis. *Inductive Preaching: Helping People Listen*. Westchester, IL: Crossway Books, 1983.

Lowry, Eugene L. *The Homiletic Plot: The Sermon as Narrative Art*. Atlanta: John Knox Press, 1980.

Robinson, Haddon. *Biblical Preaching*. Grand Rapids, MI: Baker Book House, 1980.

# Worship

Flynn, Leslie B. *Worship: Together We Celebrate*. Wheaton, IL: Victor Books, 1983.

Merrill, Dean, and Marshall Shelly, eds. *Fresh Ideas for Preaching, Worship, and Evangelism.* Christianity Today, 1984.

Ortlund, Anne. *Up With Worship.* Glendale, CA: Regal Books, 1982.

Webber, Robert. *Worship Is a Verb.* Waco, TX: Word Books, 1985.

White, James F. *Introduction to Christian Worship.* Nashville: Abingdon Press, 1980.

## Spiritual Dynamics

Cho, Paul Y. *Prayer: Key to Revival.* Waco, TX: Word Books, 1984.

Foster, Richard. *The Celebration of Discipline.* New York: Harper and Row, 1978.

Watson, David. *How to Win the War: Strategies for Spiritual Conflict.* Wheaton, IL: Harold Shaw Publishers, 1972. How Christians can be victorious in their continuing struggle to overcome their old natures and Satan's efforts to undermine them.